Bamboo & Chicke

A work of fiction that has emerged from the ten years
that the author spent living in Cambodia.

Also, from the same author
His autobiography;

"HE WENT THAT WAY"

Check out the excerpts from his interesting individual
accounts of looking for and finding the reasons as to why
the square peg does not fit into the round hole.

Excerpts can be found at the rear of this book.

Rupert Saville

Bamboo

&

Chicken Farms

Go with Bertie into Cambodia. It's his first time, he knows no one in the Kingdom and cannot speak Khmer.

Rupert Saville

-

Introduction

I have put together several large tablespoons of personal facts and experiences, to these I have added three no make that four level teaspoons of satirical writing and using a large wooden spoon mixed them all together in a bowl of my choice. Presto, I have now created the fictional character of Bertie, a retired Ships Captain.

Bertie ventures into Cambodia looking to escape the rules and regulations of political correctness and the continuing growth of Health and Safety requirements which are slowly but surely strangling the progress of mankind within the Western World.

Bertie needs to find something to keep him out of mischief. He buys a guesthouse in a small corrupt town just 8 k's inside the Cambodian / Thai border.

Bertie is a firm believer that the customer is not always right and as one can imagine this sets many scenes of interest some vocal and some bordering on let's just say a firmer approach.

His guests are varied and range from expats in Thailand doing visa runs to biker gangs and also include high flyers from the bustle of Phnom Penh seeking a weekend of fun and peace away from prying eyes and wagging tongues, let's not forget the Backpacker Brigade.

He has escaped his previous oppressive world but the small town has its own set of rules and traditions. Some are easy to adapt to, others take a little more understanding. His manageress keeps him on the straight and narrow, well most of the time and with the

*added help from Henny who runs the
"Cockadoodledo" a local Chicken Farm, (bordello)
Bertie soon becomes a well-liked and respected citizen
of Korrup Kong.*

Contents

Chapter 1

    His loving and caring mother named him Bertrand, but everyone knew him just simply as Bertie. His mother named him to honor Captain Bertrand Reginald Smithers VC. A man of great substance, courage, and loyalty that stood out above all others on their family tree. It was back in August of 1916 at the battle of the Somme that Captain Smithers had risked his life to save a small band of soldiers under his command. Alone and armed only with rifle and bayonet that he had taken from a fallen soldier that couldn't use it anymore he ran across open muddy ground strewn with dead and dying men, dead and dying horses, and scattered obstacles of barbed wire. A landscape pock marked with shell holes. Alone he dispatched four German soldiers manning a Maxim machine gun that was sure to have dealt death and destruction to his men if he had not acted quickly with little or no thought to his own safety. War is a terrible, horrific reality and made even worse as war is not fair or plays by the rules and so it was that a well-aimed but badly timed artillery shell landed and exploded in that same shell hole that Captain Smithers now occupied, killing him instantly. Some months later Captain Bertrand Reginald Smithers was posthumously awarded the Victoria Cross. That's right, war is not fair, and although only briefly mentioned it was strongly rumored that the artillery shell that took the captain's life had indeed been fired by friendly allies further to the rear.

Bertie, the Bertie who is front and center in this story is just over six feet tall and weighed in at around 220 pounds. Age had certainly added a few pounds to the waistline of Bertie. Kind of hard to visualize him as a younger man when he was a top-level rugby player and champion freestyle wrestler weighing in at 180 pounds or 80kgs.

There wasn't much that worried Bertie these days as he sat happily and contented gazing down from the window seat of the plane he had boarded in Bangkok. The partially flooded fields of rice and other crops spread neatly out below him and formed a mosaic tapestry broken by a brownish-colored ribbon of water. A ribbon of water that was obviously the dominating factor as it clearly chose its own path on its journey to join The South China Sea off the coast of Vietnam. This was the mighty Mekong, "Mother of Rivers" when translated from its internationally known Laos / Thai name.

Just another river to Bertie as he knew and understood very little about the importance of this river and its role to provide millions with sustenance and a lively hood from its very beginning on the Tibetan plateaus. This river did not discriminate between races or religions as it flowed thru China, Burma, Thailand, Lao, Cambodia and finally Vietnam after covering a distance of approximately 4500 kilometers, it reigned as mother to them all.

Until recently a big chunk of Bertie's life had been all about water, his very existence relied on water, albeit salt water with a splash of fresh thrown in just for hydration purposes. The water that filled the oceans of the world. You see Bertie was a retired ship's captain and he had experienced the oceans in all her many changing moods. He had enjoyed the calmness of her balmy nights; he had been battered and bruised when in fits of violent temper, she had threatened to smash Bertie's world into a million pieces and then as if to ask for forgiveness had been the soothing balm that restored peace and tranquility to those that sailed upon her.

However, that was all well behind him now. To keep things simple Bertie chose to think of water as being important for three, just three reasons; for the purpose of bathing; to make his morning cuppa tea; to mix with his late afternoon whiskey.

The "fasten seatbelts" overhead light flashed on in preparation for the touch down at Phnom Penh International Airport. This visit to Cambodia was a first for Bertie, although no stranger to South East Asia having spent considerable time over the past years holidaying in Thailand and working out of Singapore. Naturally he was expecting things to be similar so was quite taken back as he struggled thru the disorganized melee that was Immigration, paying an inflated price for his visa plus a little bit more because he didn't have a spare photograph even though the one in his passport showed a definite and clear resemblance to its holder.

Emerging from the front of the terminal building Bertie found himself surrounded by eager taxi drivers. Eager to know where he was going and eager to be his driver at of course the very best price. The negotiating began with an initial amount of $15.00 USD. This was a game that Bertie had played many times although not here in Cambodia. He did not let on that this was his first time and politely insisted that just a short time ago he had paid only $7.00 to take him to the same hotel in Street 172.

"But sir gasoline price goes up" they explained in unison as if trying out for the local church choir, and so it continued back and forth until finally a price of $10.00 was agreed upon. Enough time had been wasted. The lucky smiling driver placed Bertie's back pack in the boot of his shiny white taxi with the heavily tinted windows as Bertie opened the left-hand front passengers' door but came to a sudden stop as this was the driver's seat. Here in Cambodia, they drove on the right-hand side of the road. The group of taxi drivers looked on in amusement at this guy who had been here "many times" before but didn't know his left from his right. Bertie's brain kicked in with a quick reply that even surprised himself,

"Hey I pay the money so I get to drive" which added a certain amount of confusion amongst the onlookers not least of all the owner of the taxi, who breathed a sigh of relief when Bertie explained he was only joking. This in turn helped Bertie save face.

Checking in to his hotel was a simple formality and the clerk at reception barely glanced at his passport. Bertie's room was sparsely furnished with an older box TV, a noisy AC unit and an ensuite off to one side. All in all, quite acceptable as it was clean even though the walls would welcome a fresh coat of paint. The room was awarded 6 out of 10 in Bertie's estimate.

After a quick check in the bathroom mirror to ensure that his grey flat cap was at the correct angle to cover his receding hairline and that the loose shirt of

Thai silk, (you know, the one with the elephants) he wore partially hid his fast-growing paunch it was now time to stretch one's legs and drink a few beers. This was the first priority and both tasks were quickly achieved as Bertie made himself comfortable in the nearby Kandal markets. A busy hive of activity where one could buy almost anything from the massive assortment of goods on display and more than likely goods of a dubious nature not on display, but could be quickly provided if you knew the right people to talk to.

Bertie was on his 3rd bottle of Angkor beer when his curiosity began to get the better of him. The whole idea of coming to Cambodia was to get away from the pressures and fast-growing PC bullshit, the entangled mess of rules and regulations fast threatening to drown the western world, so why couldn't Bertie just let sleeping dogs lie. He mentally promised himself, a promise he could easily break as no one else knew of it, but if he could just solve this puzzle then he would stick to his intentions and let the world continue to spin and self-destruct without his interference. Bertie was puzzled by the number of men in civilian clothing, wearing no formal means of identification that were aimlessly wandering about the stalls. The one noticeable thing they had in common was the AK47s they had slung from their shoulders, hadn't the problems with the Khmer Rouge ended some 30 years ago?

Approaching the closest of these armed men Bertie introduced himself, his reply was just a toothless smile as him with the gun couldn't understand a word of what Bertie had spoken. Not to be outdone or fobbed off Bertie like a dog with a bone between his teeth pressed on with his verbal interrogation, "Is your gun a real gun" still no reply "do you have bullets for your gun" at this stage a nearby friendly Khmer women who had a sound understanding of the English language decided she had better help Bertie out. It was plain for all to see except Bertie himself that him with the gun was starting to get just a wee bit agitated. However, Bertie still wanted answers and pressed on with his questions "are the bullets for your gun real and how many bullets do you have" this prompted a short verbal exchange between the kind lady and him with the gun who then moved off and was soon lost in the crowd. The lady with a great deal of patience then explained that yes the bullets were very real and that he had a completely full magazine so its best you stay well clear of men armed with fully loaded AK47's in this part of town.

Jostling along in the Tuk-tuk bound for Street 104 Bertie muttered to himself "I bet that daft bugger couldn't hit the side of a barn with his pop gun, full magazine or not" then suddenly he checked himself. Whilst it was sort of ok to make silent promises to himself that no one but he knew about, this talking to himself seemed to be on the increase over the past few months and the volume was determined by just what it was Bertie was discussing with himself so it had to stop. Easier said than done because more often than not he was well into the discussion before it actually became apparent to him and anyone within close proximity that Bertie was speaking to only himself. Certainly, a project to be worked on in the days ahead.

Now it was decision time. Can life not be free of decisions? Wouldn't it be nice everything laid out, all the pieces in their proper places, like some English breakfast table in a fine historic hotel? Fat chance of that ever happening and besides Bertie was out to set himself free of conformity so he needed to stand alone and make these decisions even if they may turn out to be life threatening or perhaps at the very least cause some form of physical discomfort.

So, upon alighting from his Tuk-tuk, what bar to visit first? Rose bar or Oscars? Should he toss a coin? Alas no easy way out there as all Riel, Cambodian currency consisted only of notes.

It didn't really matter as the evening was still young and the numerous bars that lined both sides of Street 104 all looked pretty much the same. The obvious difference at first glance was clearly just the names that flashed in brightly lit neon's, some only partially lit but all being in splendid competition with each other. It was Rose or Oscars that Bertie now searched for. Two bars referred to him in a smoky dimly lit bar on a back Soi in Patpong, Thailand some months previously.

Casting glances up and down the street at the many signs with his good eye. Yes, the one he used most of the time as the eye on the right had been of little use since its inception. A prime example of a lazy eye that despite several attempts to correct its lazy habits had shrugged off these attempts as it preferred to be of no real use but no big deal as Rose bar soon appeared off to the left.

A gaggle of four scantily dressed girls adorned the entrance but the night had only just begun and so with purpose Bertie strode past the girls and swung open the entrance door. More girls sat at intervals along the bar which owned the right-hand side of the interior and serviced the punters and the freelance ladies of the night with cold beers or a mixed abundance of high-level octane beverages designed to weaken any resistance or pretense that one was only there for a liquid refreshment. The opposing side was an arrangement of partially closed booths some fulfilling their purpose and providing sanctuary for couples engaged in some heavy petting while others provided an observation post for keen eyed girls eager to share the small space with hopefully a punter with time to kill and money to spend. The rear area was occupied by a pool table and hopefully but not plain to see some place where a man could release pressure on an uncomfortable bladder caused by perhaps an over indulgence of either Angkor or Anchor beer.

Bertie acknowledged the sweet smiles and hellos but was non-committal in any further communications as he was longing for an undisturbed cold beer and to just take in the sights that surrounded him. Making himself comfortable on a black plastic and chrome barstool that squealed in protest as he adjusted his weight for the maximum in comfort, he lit an Ara Red which he had taken from the soft pack he kept in his shirt pocket. Crossing his mind were thoughts of a promise he had made on the eve of a new year and had been a repeated promise on the eve of several new year's since then, but what the hell it was one of those promises that no one else knew about. He dragged deeply on the little white soldier, perhaps his one and only crutch in life, perhaps.

Finding Oscars was easy and after passing numerous bars of which all looked pretty much the same, all sporting several appealing and smiling hostesses beckoning those passing by in to sample the delights that "only "their bar could offer……. The difference at Oscars was it was not narrow gutted with a pool table furnishing the rear. Oscars was closer to being square with no pool table but room for a small dance floor which added interest to Bertie's adventure. After partaking in several beers, he loved to dance up close and personal and there certainly were no shortage of dancing partners whom kept Bertie and his wallet constantly in strong demand. The Sitabout and Taties could wait until tomorrow.

He awoke early on the morning of the morrow and was soon seated at one of the hotels three street side tables. His attention and concentration captured by a freshly poured cup of tea and his 2nd cigarette of the day glowed a deep red in the chipped and cracked sea shell that had been forced into early retirement as an ashtray.

Bertie loved his eggs on toast with the white cooked firm and the yolk still runny so was disappointed when in due course and just as he had begun his 3rd cigarette that his breakfast arrived. The whites and yolks were extremely well cooked to the point where one could throw these eggs as one would throw a frisbee. The local street dogs would then be able to chase and fetch but not return as your new frisbee would disappear in a swirl of contrasting colored dog hairs accompanied by a mixture of barks, yelps and finally a deep growl claiming possession.

It was a short walk of about 15 minutes that took him to the National Museum of Cambodia. A walk that took him past numerous eateries many displaying chalk boards advertising the universally known "All Day Breakfast" and Bertie pondered to himself that whoever wrote that first advertisement would and maybe even did make a substantial fortune if he indeed had been able to put a patent on it. One small restaurant had even gone one better than the chalk board and displayed a sign with the use of small different colored flashing torch bulbs, however some had blown and gone un-noticed so the flickering sign did read "All Da- B- - akfa-t" ("All Da Bakfat" for those of you that are not the sharpest knife in the drawer) Passing customers may consider that the vendor was selling an alternative to Pork Belly.

Arriving a little early Bertie had time to wander around the gardens of the museum. A pleasant stroll and time to think of the massive amount of human labor hours it would have required for construction to have taken place back in 1920. During the years from 1975 to 1979 it was evacuated and abandoned due to the Khmer Regime after which it was restored once a cauldron of bats that had taken sanctuary during those horrific and terrible times had been removed.

Just as Bertie was approaching the entrance door a 12-seater minivan screeched to a halt directly in his path. A side door was slide open and out scrambled not 12 but 18 noisy chattering mix of male and female Chinese tourists all of whom were totally oblivious to Bertie's presence. The small and somewhat insignificant tour guide then managed not without considerable effort to form this mass of inconsiderate humans into a somewhat orderly group and directed them in thru the entrance doors. For quite some time after the last one had disappeared from sight their loud high-pitched voices could be heard echoing thru out the confines of this once peaceful representation of Cambodian history.

So it was that Bertie cancelled his museum trip not trusting himself to behave as a gentleman if he should enter and find himself face to face with such a selfish rabble.

Prior to his trip to Cambodia Bertie had read up and asked various questions hoping to gain some qualified information and understanding of how it was for the Kingdoms majority population to live, to die, to lose loved ones, to barely survive under Pol Pot and his henchmen. The information he gathered was more than enough for him to have a deep respect for those that had endured and suffered and a personal hatred for those responsible for this genocide. Enough was enough for Bertie and with these thoughts in mind he passed on going to visit Tuol Sleng Genocide Museum, formally the Security Prison 21 (S-21) or out to The Killing Fields.

A couple of cold beers back at Kandal market followed by an extended walk along the riverside and he was at the Virak Buntan bus office where for $7.00 he purchased a ticket for the following days trip down to the coastal town of Sihanoukville.

Motor bike taxi's and Tuk-tuks were extremely cheap, $1.00 / $1.50 could get you anywhere within the downtown area, however relying on his trustee shanks pony it wasn't long before he passed thru the entrance of the Sitabout pub on street 51.

Notorious and as some journalists described as "Cambodia's seediest pub" its reputation was spread far and wide. The description was not unfounded as Bertie found himself in the midst of a colorful selection of freelance prostitutes and an assortment of expats and or sex tourists many under the influence of severe intoxication and or effects of nonprescription drugs. The age group beginning from mid-twenties and spiraling upwards into infinity. A human tide that ebbed and flowed. The underlying currents consisting of directional glances. Glances that ran parallel with the timber bar. Glances of acute and obtuse angles that crisscrossed and bisected the entire area. Glances that were acknowledged and returned with smiles of acceptance, or frowns of rejection, but whatever the response it did all seem to work. The smokey air hung like a thin morning fog over the assembled and slow-moving patrons and somehow unknowingly kept the noise to a level where conversation was possible, broken only when a poorly played shot on the pool table caused the white ball to leap from the table, crash on the timber / tiled floor and roll several meters as if attempting to escape. Only to be captured and returned to a position within the D from where play could recommence and the single white ball could continue to send the numerous coloreds down the holes that they had come out of. White won even though always the underdog, the odds against white 15 to 1 at start of play. No matter the odds white always won.

A great place for quick relationships to be formed and often extended to the upstairs short time rooms. A number of these romances proved that climbing the stairs followed by further physical activities invigorated with the addition of Cialis proved just too much for some in the older age bracket, resulting in them being removed from the premises in the horizontal position and driven to the city morgue. Many would argue that there was no better way to die, certainly a subject that was discussed in detail when the news that yet another had fallen drifted down to the bar below.

Bertie mused to himself that he was far too young and had much more to do before he took that particular stairway to heaven. Please note he mused these thoughts and did not mutter out loud and to himself as so far today he had managed to keep the audio track on his thoughts turned down to the volume that only he could hear.

Late afternoon was approaching so after buying one more drink for the female companion that had self-invited herself to his table and for the last hour been unsuccessful in her attempts to whisk him away to her nearby room, he bade her farewell and walked albeit with a bit of a stagger to the street outside and in to the collection of eager motorbike taxi drivers.

Shanks pony had done their share for the day so it was on the back of a motor bike that Bertie perched himself rather precariously with knees tucked in tightly as they buzzed, rattled and dodged traffic of all descriptions. Traffic that came and went from all directions but this noisy smoky chaos worked extremely well. That little jaunt seemed to have a sobering effect on Bertie so it was outside Taties in Street 130 that he paid his fare and faced the daunting stairway that led up to the bar and hopefully a great Tex Mex dinner.

The stairway was extremely steep rising up perhaps 30 steps, maybe more. The treads were narrow and shallow accommodating perhaps only half the length of a normal foot, the stairway coming down was exactly the same. How could it be otherwise as one entered and left using that one and only stairway. Of course, those of you that have been fed and entertained in Taties will well be able to recall and picture that flight of stairs.

The climb was worth the effort. Easy listening live music was provided by a single entertainer with promises of a four-piece band taking the stage at about 9.00pm. The seating was comfortable and well-spaced with several opportunities to view the street below from outside decks. The menu was varied and looked tempting but did not list prices and alternative specials of the day that could be provided by an assortment of friendly smiling freelancers. One could say with respect of course that the assortment here was slightly more upmarket than what was on offer at the Sitabout.

Bertie enjoyed a few drinks and a tasty meal of chicken and beans before retiring rather early as the following day he was off to Sihanoukville.

Chapter 2

Bertie was well ahead of the eight ball despite a frustrating look for his bus ticket which he eventually found in the pocket of the shirt he had worn the day before "you know the one with the printed water buffalo's, which was very similar to the one with the printed elephants and if pushed in to a corner then he would have to admit that the elephant shirt was his favorite but he couldn't wear that every day as people would begin to talk"

He had just finished his 2nd cup of tea, make no mistake there were no fried egg Frisbee's for the scavenging hounds on this fine morning. He was on his fourth cigarette when the mini bus pulled up to take him and several other passengers already onboard for the short ride to the main bus terminal. Here they bordered a larger bus and headed off on a stop start journey thru the bustling and increasing number of the city's morning commuters.

Passing thru the industrial area of sweat shops and huge foreign owned garment factories the rubbish on both sides of the road steadily grew and overflowed into the large monsoon drains running parallel to the sealed road upon which the bus was travelling as it slowly increased in speed and made its way out into the countryside. The bus driver would use any excuse to sound the horn not that the cows that wandered wherever they pleased upon this busy thoroughfare took any notice. The horn seemed to be the conductor of the interior's orchestra, closely followed by the loud Khmer movie being shown on the overhead screen and the passengers were certainly not going to be outdone as they continued with raised voices to talk on a variety of cell phones to those they had just left behind or perhaps to warn those further down the track that they had indeed left Phnom Penh and were on their way.

Comfort stops were frequent and due to the lack of proper roadside convenience's these would consist of pulling over to the shoulder of the road where once off the bus the males would point their peckers away from the bus and do what comes naturally. The females would squat where ever they felt most comfortable some seeking privacy behind a low solitary bush creating a scene which when helped with a small amount of imagination one could visualize perhaps a picture of different colored mushrooms waiting to be picked seen as an illustration one would expect to see in an infant's story book.

The passengers were not all Khmers so to some of the foreigner's this practice came as a bit of a surprise or even shock. Hushed whispers and audible comments passed between some passengers whilst others preferred to keep their thoughts to themselves,

"I might find some privacy behind that nearby bush but can the people on the bus still see me"

"Don't look now but that man over there is facing the wrong way and holding it with both hands, he does seem to be enjoying himself"

"No worries, Garry, it's just fucking good not to be a Sheila eh buddy"

Which comment fits where? I will rely on you to decide.

Those of you with an average IQ would have now come to the conclusion that the bus although noisy and air-conditioned does not have an onboard toilet. For those of you who are not perhaps the brightest bulb in the chandelier then don't fret as you still have a couple of hours to come to this conclusion before the bus reaches its final destination.

Passing thru small villages where most houses were built on stilts so as to remain dry during the monsoon season Bertie was pleasantly surprised and equally impressed to see the young children in smart and clean school uniforms. The boys in white shirts and blue shorts the girls in white blouses and ankle length blue pleated skirts. They lined the roadside as many walked hands in hand with brothers, sisters or good friends. There was no sexual illustration attached to who held hands with who and to those that looked out from behind the buses windows then none was made and perhaps thoughts were formed as to why children with so very little could radiate such happiness and wholesome trust. Cambodia's children of today, Cambodia's future adults.

However, Bertie was not so naïve that he did not know there are always two sides to every coin. The reverse side of this coin was scarred and tarnished and reflected thousands of Khmer families that lived on or well below the poverty line. Young and old, male and female forced to live and beg on the streets that offered little in return, to search thru rubbish at nearby dumps for anything that may possibly be resold, to forage for thrown away food that may possibly still be eatable. Young children of both sexes forced into prostitution, some before they have even reached puberty. What sort of low life parasitic scumbags once again of both sexes have the right to force their despicable cravings and fetishes on those so very young and to capitalize on the misfortunes of others. These very children are also the rightful and important future adults of Cambodia. Bertie knew very well what he would do if he should ever come across anyone that without effort or thought can and do threaten and terrorize those so young. I am sure many of you readers would also be in the front line along with numerous groups and organizations that are currently fighting tooth and nail to secure a brighter, a better future for those that thru no fault of their own are less fortunate.

Pulling into the poor excuse for a bus station and before the bus had stopped a group of perhaps 15 or more Tuk-tuk drivers and motor bike taxi drivers scrambled to be first in line and to attach themselves to the front door of the bus as others jostled for position forming a caterpillar like line as they trotted beside the slow-moving bus which did eventually come to a stop. All of them being hopeful to get a fare as the passengers physically forced themselves thru this human wall and to vacant areas beyond. Yes, room now to breathe but certainly not without being constantly pestered by those that had been unsuccessful just minutes before.

"FREEDOM" I can imagine this word would bring back to many the scene where Mel Gibson playing the part of William Wallace in the movie "Braveheart" screamed out that very word as he was hung drawn and quartered. I will tell you no more. If you want to know more than do your own research as this is not a history lesson relating to the escapades and adventures of "Wee Willie Wallace", this is instead a recollection of the escapades and adventures of "Big Bold Bertie" during his time in The Kingdom of Cambodia.

Freedom awakened no such memories for Bertie. Freedom was simply the name of the hotel he was now looking for which was located not far from the bus stop in central downtown Sihanoukville. It was a relatively easy place to find. It was bloody good to be away from that awful damn bus stop with its over congested atmosphere. It was even better to be leaning against the downstairs bar of the Freedom supping on a nice cold beer even though each sip or swallow was interrupted by some freelance lady hoping to tempt Bertie to a game of pool on one of the three tables. Game of pool oh just the ice breaker for possible things to come but he would have none of it, maybe later. In the meantime, just to be left alone, drink his beer and smoke a cigarette or two was all he wanted right there and then. Mind you in taking all that in to account he did most certainly take note of that really pretty one with the very short dress that kept leaning at provocative angles over the nearest pool table mmmmm definitely maybe later.

Having chilled his internal workings with the contents of several cans of Angkor beer and reinstated his nicotine dependency to the required level, Bertie tore himself away from the bar and pretty pool player and checked in. That all took only about 15 minutes and then true to form he was back propping up the bar in the same spot as before. Unbeknown to everyone, but this was now Bertie's spot. Well according to the good book that Bertie wrote it was now his that is until he found a better spot with a better view of all three pool tables and the scantily dressed girls that plied their trade with not so innocent gestures using que and balls like an actor would perhaps use stage props to engage his eager and enthusiastic audience.

Time for a change of scenery, well not so much the scenery but the location. Somewhere on previous travels in distant places someone had suggested if he ever got to Sihanoukville then a relatively short street up at Victory Hill was well worth a look. Ok no need for further encouragement and after securing the fare with one of numerous motor bike taxis Bertie clambered aboard and holding on tightly was spirited away hopefully to the street he was looking for.

It just so happened that the driver of this ancient motorbike that Bertie hung on tightly to...... well he had a very good friend who ran a very good bar in this very good street so guess what? Yep, right first time. That's where the two wheeled wanders came to a bumpy stop directly right out front of this very good bar. Who the fuck needs a guide book when there are all these very good friends one can rely on?

The bar was comfortable, the beer was cold and the lighting was not too bright or the music too noisy. The compliment of hostess girls was perhaps a little full in one's face but Bertie soon set up his perimeters and conditions if indeed he was to spend some time in this particular bar as the small street was made up of bars, bottle to bottle, wall to wall, shoulder to shoulder and they all competed for sales of beverages, girls and unnamed substances. Bertie muttered to himself "a small version of Soi Six in Pattaya, Thailand" then quickly checked himself as he had been doing so well in keeping his talking to himself under control.

The street outside was rough and unsealed. Someone or something at one time had spread a meagre scattering of small stones in various areas but these in no way managed to fill the abundance of potholes spread along the streets entire length forming no particular pattern. It had begun to rain and puddles soon formed to replace the dry cavities. Neon lights threw their colors upon those puddles which turned into shimmering reflections and simply added to the mystique and attraction of this small street.

After dodging rain drops and striding over and around these saucers of bizarre imagery Bertie struck up conversation with a hostess from the bar, he now found himself in. It wasn't long before the offer although verbal but with the sincerest promise that he would be safe and there would be no more to pay Bertie allowed himself to be led, to be guided to a small room down an unlit walkway. Had Bertie walked into a trap? It was extremely dark in this small room and on his prompted tour from the bar, perhaps his last bastion of safety, he had noticed figures lurking in and around the shadows of adjacent rooms. Bertie's apprehension slowly eased at about the same speed as the flame from the candle his new found friend had lit spread its yellowish light throughout this musty haven. This meagre glow exposed just one single mattress upon the earthen floor, and to be practical what else was needed as support for a massage with a happy ending to be performed. Let's give the mattress a little bit of credit as it did look in quite good condition, but was it a permanent home for differing species of any number of insects and associated creepy crawlies? Bertie had come this far and was not about to back out now so pushing thoughts of centipedes, fire ants and such to the very back of his alcohol induced brain he stretched out on this mattress and subjected himself to a surprisingly good massage, and a surprisingly great happy ending with no further extra costs asked for.

Gently but firmly, he was ushered out the door and into the dark damp expanse beyond. It was there that he stood as the door was closed, not slammed in his face but firmly closed and there was no mistaking the sound of a security bolt being slid into place. Why was she remaining behind? As there was no need to make up the bed with non-existing sheets or flush a non-existing toilet. Bertie only knew that he was alone in the darkness. Where was the lady with the lamp / candle when he needed her most? Behind a closed and bolted door was where she was. Was it now that the trap would be sprung? Oh, for fucks sake Bertie stop imagining things and get out of the darkness and back in to civilization, and that's exactly what he did and as fast as he possibly could.

Now back in the relative safety of the first bar that Bertie came to on his flight from the darkness he quickly ordered a double scotch with just a dash of water and downed it in record time, followed at a slightly slower pace by a 2nd and then a 3rd These helped to ease his shaky nerves and enabled him to resume the appearance of someone that had everything totally under control, allowing him to light up cigarettes that he thankfully dragged deeply on. These

Ara Red were a pretty good smoke and at about 30 cents for a pack of 20 Bertie was quick to form what he hoped would be a long and lasting friendship with this band of white soldiers. There now things are not that bad, are they?

Outside the rain had not eased so it was a Tuk-tuk that delivered him back to Freedom and the only just acceptable noise of the resident band. During his absence they must have had a crew change because the girls that were now around, on, or under the pool tables certainly seemed an older selection and several of the smiling faces were betrayed where mascara and or lipstick had failed to hide the signs of time. One more double scotch just to help him up the stairs and he was off to bed as it was beach day tomorrow.

With a gigantic effort Bertie managed to shake off the numerous dreams that had plagued his sleep by waking and then reviving himself in a cold shower which could have, would have been a blessing had it been more than an apologetic drizzle that stopped and started to its own unwritten schedule. Stepping from the shower the rise in his level of consciousness allowed him to fully realize that yes morning had arrived and his wristwatch further alerted him that it was now 8.35am. Fuck what was in those drinks, how many had he drank as it was highly unusual and a little scary to wake so late. Settle down and don't get agitated he told himself as it wasn't as if his ship was sailing at 0845hrs or any other time, no those days were well behind him.

It didn't take long for him to find a small shop house that knocked up a bowl of spicy pork mince and rice resulting in a cross between a soup and a porridge and once consumed was a great and quick fixer of hangovers. After scraping the bowl clean of the very last grain of rice Bertie studied his guide booklet as he needed to make a decision, an informed decision as to which beach his primary target would be. Bertie had to surrender and agree, yes, some tourist guide books are quite useful.

There were several to choose from and this proved to be a time of personnel exposure because he did get into quite a loud and audible discussion with himself as to which beach would better suit his needs. The young waitress actually thought he was ordering a second serving and became quite embarrassed when she placed the fresh bowl in front of Bertie only to have him politely decline the hot bowl of fix me up, one was sufficient thank you.

Several cigarettes and a chilled can of beer later brought Bertie to the unanimous decision that Serendipity actually part of the long stretch of white sand that made up Ochheuteal Beach would be the one for him. Thanking his hosts and leaving a more than generous tip for the helpful but still embarrassed waitress he made his way down the dodgy and unevenly paved walkway that could have passed for a footpath if only the obstacles of pushbikes, motorbikes, rubbish bins and a multitude of other household items had not made it their place of casual or permanent residence.

Too far to walk on this particular morning so with some effort and repeatedly pointing to relevant pictures in his guide book Bertie was soon again perched on the back of a motorbike as they rounded the Golden Lion roundabout and minutes later found himself standing on a road running parallel to the white sandy beach.

Between him and the water's edge was an assortment of thatched huts fulfilling the purpose of eateries and bars or in many cases both. This collection seemed to run the entire length of the beach and did indeed look promising in being able to supply cold beers including a multitude of other liquid refreshments, plus food to fortify the soul. Brilliant thought Bertie exactly what he was looking for. Thank you so much my informative and loyal guide book, he muttered quietly.

Once on the beach he kicked off his sandals and immediately felt the warm grains of white sand underfoot, a soothing and welcoming feeling, and with his now fast approaching relaxed attitude Bertie just knew this was going to be a good day.

There was an endless collection of various multi colored reclining seats constructed of canvas on timber frames, interrupted only by a similar variety of sun umbrella's that seemed to form a line of defense between the clear rippling waters of the sea and the thatched huts. Some huts now belting out songs that seemed to marry well with the surroundings. That is to say no rap or heavy metal stuff. Oh, it was there, stored on the shelves below the bars and would play their part late in the afternoon and on thru the night when the younger sect would invade like fire flies this once tranquil setting.

Bertie didn't hesitate in choosing an orange-colored recliner as these he noted were less in number and seemed to have been positioned in solitary spots where the blue, white and red recliners were grouped together in their distinct colors as if forming their very own gangs. He had been and still was a strong backer of the underdog so it was orange that he was backing today. He dared anyone should attempt to change his mind and with a great show of ownership he adjusted his orange companion to suit his comfort.

This was the life and that was about where his train of thought was when interrupted by an elderly lady requesting a rental fee for occupying one of her recliners and upon producing a poorly laminated plastic menu from her apron pocket indicated if she could get him something to eat and or drink. Definitely no need to be asked twice about something to drink he pointed at the faded picture of a can of Angkor and dismissed its neighboring pictures of fish, prawns and other assorted dishes. Time enough for food once he sorted his thirst as the day was certainly warming up. Who knows a few more cans and Bertie may even venture in for a swim? Possible but highly unlikely!!

Totally relaxed, he found himself in his own little world. His little world of peace and satisfaction. No more shipping deadlines to meet, no more wild and savage storms to battle and yes that head and shoulder massage about an hour ago by a girl of about 18 had most definitely helped him reach this level of euphoria. Hey, hey let's not forget the added help of perhaps six cans of beer or was it eight. Who cares? Bertie wasn't telling anyone and neither should you.

Bertie had no use for the small trinkets made of plastic or shell that young children offered for sale. He preferred to tip them for their efforts, secretly hoping that the few thousand riel he parted with did actually be of help and was not used to buy alcohol or drugs for controlling adults who may be out of sight but close by and keeping a keen watch on their young wards.

Several days past and each day and evening routine remained pretty much the same. Days at the beach and evenings plus a few very late nights in bars up on Victory Hill. There was another interest that Bertie pursued. How he managed to fit this extra activity into his busy schedule of beaches and bars surprised his new found friends but fit it in he did. Bertie knew that it was only a matter of time before he would become bored so he needed some sort of job or maybe even a business to keep him occupied and the wolves from his door.

After talking and asking questions to anyone that would listen, he did eventually build a picture and dug a well, albeit a somewhat shallow well of knowledge about the local community and a wider understanding of just how the system would allow a foreigner to indeed operate within the very loose structure of their business laws. There was an abundance of bars run by expats and several were for sale but Bertie required something slightly more substantial and so he set about searching for a guesthouse combined with bar and restaurant.

Finding something suitable was proving more difficult than he first thought. He was disappointed at the low standard of building maintenance that was poorly hidden behind perhaps an appealing frontage. He was disappointed at the just about nonexistence of any form of book keeping. The general attitude amongst the foreign operators seemed to be as long as they had money in their pocket at the end of the week then why bother with all that other stuff and it became obvious, they had not come to work. They had come to play. Some were that dumb or totally confused by an over indulgence in alcohol and or drugs that they believed because they owned the business then the commodities, they sold such as food and drink was free to them. They would surely be able to put forward an argument that Santa Clause was indeed true. An argument that was totally flawed to anyone with half a brain that is. Be that as it may but no way was Bertie investing in any enterprise of any description if some sort of trading record could be produced. Of course, he was very well aware that books can be and do get doctored or cooked but the evidence of some sort of record valid or invalid did throw some reflection that the current owner actually did show some interest in the management of his business.

Several weeks passed and a number of possibilities were visited some of which were dismissed without a second thought others lasted perhaps a full 24 hours before being simply struck off the list. Bertie was beginning to think that what he was looking for just didn't exist and that his idea would not come to fruition.

It was one evening when supporting the weight of the bar and in his usual spot watching the pool balls rolling in all directions following unsuccessful shots from unsuccessful ladies that Bertie just happened to hear two expats discussing that their friend up in Korrup Kong had his business up for sale.

Could this be the one? So politely he introduced himself and asked the necessary questions. The answers were to his liking and without much prompting he learnt, yes it was a guesthouse with bar, restaurant and a small swimming pool, but where the fuck was Korrup Kong? Well, these two guys had all the information as they were probably hoping for a spotter's fee from the current owner so without being prompted, they informed Bertie that Korrup Kong was a delightful small town about 8 k's from the Thai Cambodian border and they went on to offer a contact phone number and then bid their goodnight but not before asking Bertie to make sure when talking to the seller that it was indeed Sid & Cyril from down in Snooky that had told him about it.

Following a restless night, as his thought were invaded by visions of this delightful town close to the border, at 8am an hour he figured to be polite he placed the call. Yes, the business was still for sale and he agreed to catch the bus to Korrup Kong the very next day.

Bertie was quite excited and spent the remainder of the day getting a massage on the beach from his favored masseuse promising he would return one day and finally ordering a combination fried rice along with several beers from the old lady with the worn-out menu.

Chapter 3

The bus journey to Korrup Kong lasted nearly five hours and had all the entertainment of the noisy bus horn, Khmer films and loud talking passengers plus the colorful comfort stops along the way. Yes, that's correct just a copycat version of his previous bus trip but Bertie did enjoy the scenery of the rainforests as they passed thru the Cardamom mountains. He even spotted a troupe of maybe six or seven monkeys on the side of the road simply doing what monkeys' do. Quite an improvement from some of the "wildlife" he had found himself in company with since his arrival in Cambodia.

It soon became obvious to Bertie as the bus slowly made its way down what appeared to be the main street that Korrup Kong was not a big town. The word small springs to mind but the street was surprisingly very busy. The male population choosing to travel on fairly ancient motor bikes whilst the ladies of the town seemed happy and contented to go about their business on push bikes and wearing what Bertie could only describe as brightly colored pyjama's and either cone shaped hats of some woven fiber or cotton sun bonnets.

Pyjama's, his mind flashed back to his first wife, or was it his second? He had had on his last count a total of three and each of them were now all past their expiry date. No one can blame him for forgetting who was responsible for this flash back but flash back it certainly was and not pleasant in fact very disturbing. Wife number two certainly was the worst so it must have been her who would come waltzing into the bedroom dressed in her red and white striped flannelette pyjama's' hoping for a night of wild passion now he had returned from six weeks at sea. Seeing this image of a dying love and past hopes never realized approaching on a definite collision course with little hope of escape Bertie had no choice but to surrender and as wife number two had her wicked way all Bertie could think of is that it wouldn't be so bad if she didn't wear those fucking flannelette pyjamas'. He expanded on that and thought that next time he came home she will have her hair in curlers and be wearing sheepskin slippers, and that's when Bertie set out in earnest to find his third wife.

Shaking off those terrible memories he was intrigued by just how attractive many of these local women seemed to be, but what seems to be the hold up as the bus came to rather an abrupt stop, oh nothing more than some local farmer crossing the road leading his water buffalo that in turn pulled a cart loaded with some type of green vegetation.

Many passengers had got to their feet and had begun sorting out their treasured belongings so the bus stop must be close. Was it a coincidence or simply good luck but whatever the bus pulled up and stopped right outside the guesthouse Bertie had come to look at? Of course, there was the usual struggle thru a mass of arms and legs some of which belonged to fellow passengers and some to locals hoping to secure a fare of some description or another before Bertie could find breathing space and orientate himself.

The guesthouse owner must have warned his staff of his pending arrival as before he had time to light a cigarette a young lady approached him and asked him if he was Mr. Bertie. Acknowledging the fact that indeed he was this young lady whom spoke very good English requested he follow her to meet the owner who was having his afternoon beer out the back by the pool. Lazy fucker, why couldn't the owner be there to meet him in person and this attitude did not sit well with Bertie. Bertie had a short fuse when it came to bad manners or inconsideration for others, so off to a bumpy start. Awkward introductions were passed around with Bertie finding it hard to accept this seemingly somewhat hostile attitude and he was very close to explode and quite possibly throw the prick into the pool when begrudgingly a curved ball came his way in the guise of a cold beer being offered and just as well that it was cold because it did reduce Bertie's temperature a few degrees. He was now able to concentrate on his reason for being there.

Bertie asks the questions and replies came slowly, fuck a bit like pulling teeth. The only real sign of any energy from the owner came when he rang the bell to summon the young lady to bring another beer. Was she the only staff member? Then as if from nowhere a Thai woman appeared and spoke rapidly and loudly to Bertie's sparring partner who between drinks seemed to hold the position of being her husband, then just as quickly she disappeared. Thank fuck for that as it was obvious, she wore the pants.

As bits and pieces of information came forth and sentences were put together Bertie realized the owner was also a Kiwi and came from New Zealand. A small country located way down under and not far from Australia. The latest five yearly census showed NZ to have a population of around 3.5 million humans and twice as many sheep. The census gathered a wide scope of information and was designed to help the country's infrastructure keep pace with its growth. Fairly simple forms to fill in but some people stumbled when asked where they were born and what was their date of birth. There were a number of councilors ready and able to help thru these stressful questions. No need to give their age as due to the recent shipment of calculators arriving in Wellington, NZ's capitol city then those reviewing the information were allocated said calculators and could after extensive tuition in their use subtract date of birth from the current date and work out the age of the informant and this just reinforced how clever some of these Kiwis were.

Councilors? A government picked team of specially trained learned people strategically placed in and around NZ's trouble spots. So called experts in all facets of human behavior and emotional reactions to adverse conditions and normally faced with a five-day week, nine to five hours of employment. However, this could rapidly change and perhaps the best example of this was when NZ's top team of rugby union players known as the CD's (Country's Dancers) faced a huge loss to their trans-Tasman rivals the Wannabies. The final score being 68 to 3 and to make matters worse and increase the speed that the wave of depression swept the entire country the game was played at Eden

Park the very home, the very heart of NZ rugby. This brought about unprecedented pressure upon the councilors whom after several days began themselves to break down and now the councilors were in need of being counselled. One would say a bit of a problem now faced the governing powers and at last report they were still debating on just what they could do.

Hold up, this is not about the age of Kiwis or how the loss of a simple game can have such disastrous effects, nor is it about how many sheep you can get in to a telephone box, a difficult question as the calculators having come from South Korea had little or no built-in knowledge of what this sheep thing was. So, let's get back to Bertie by the pool.

There had been progress and it was agreed that Bertie would take a poolside room for the next fortnight. He would spend this time monitoring the business and going over the company's trading figures which the Thai wife had forcefully dumped on the small table. The same table also supported cans of beer which showed their displeasure at sharing the small space by frothing up and over the top. One could almost hear them crying out in a bubbly voice "bitch" and Bertie couldn't agree more with his little aluminum friends.

One must give credit where credit is due and Joy the Thai wife had kept an excellent record of all business transactions during the three years of ownership. Bertie spent several days reviewing and cross checking all relevant entries. They were set out in neat and readable notation and certainly seemed to balance, but of course no guarantee as it became apparent that Joy was no fool and it would have been easily possible for her to "cook the books" but at least it showed there was an interest in the business.

There was no benefit in showing false figures for taxation purposes as tax was not calculated on loss or profit of revenue. The amount of tax paid was simply dependent on the total number of rooms in the guesthouse and how many seats were available in the restaurant and bar, in complete disregard to the revenue created or lost by these rooms and the seating arrangement.

He also spent different times of the day and night just watching and listening to the everyday activities and it soon became apparent that Leroy the owner did very little and he also stood out as a bully. This trait was illustrated clearly by his raised and angry voice when speaking to any of the five staff members especially the small one that seemed to do all the work. Bertie noticed that poor girl was also often in the firing line of Joys fiery temper tantrums as well and for the life of him he could only find praise and respect for her as he watched her go about her chores with a smile and happy demeanor.

One morning whilst sitting poolside sipping on his cup of tea all hell broke loose in the kitchen and by the sounds of things frying pans and saucepans were fast becoming airborne. Going on the vocals and noise of battle it seemed as if Leroy and Joy had locked horns on yet another occasion. Guess who got the blame. Can you? If you had been paying attention then no prizes if your pick of the five staff members was none other than the small one. Yes of course it was Mir, the smallest of them all. This time it was more than she could handle and simply fled the war zone with tears in her eyes that she could not hide as she passed close to Bertie. He despised bullies so set off and followed Mir, not the easiest task as she was making good speed on her bicycle and Bertie was soon finding himself short of breath. Keeping her in sight he was able to see her reach the ramshackle room of timber and corrugated iron that she shared with her mother and the place she called home.

Mir and her Mum were seated outside on a low wooden bench just to the right of the entrance door that hung at a slight but noticeable angle in a weak show of protection for the room's small interior. Would it be impolite to intrude? Bertie asked himself. He had met Mir's mum on a previous occasion so he pushed forward in what he hoped would be a polite and respectful intrusion. No need to be concerned as they both welcomed him moving aside to make room for him on this one solitary piece of furniture.

What followed was a simple but sincere offer from Bertie asking Mir to come and work for him if indeed he should go ahead and buy the business. Mir's face brightened and her characteristic smile supported her positive reply and yes, she would be very happy to work for Bertie. That's all good then and after a general chat and a drink of tepid water from a galvanized iron mug Bertie logged Mir's phone number and assured her, he would be in touch.

Bertie was feeling good about the business and was quite sure that he would soon make an offer, but before he got to that stage, he had some investigative homework to do around the small town. During the next few days, he asked what appeared as innocent questions to various expats and also local market vendors that supplied pork, chicken and an assortment of vegetables to the guesthouse. One of the most useful and repetitive comments he received was that Leroy and Joy were desperate to sell as Joy had had enough of small Cambodian towns and wanted to return to her family in Thailand. The big bully Leroy as was common with bullies had no real backbone to stand alone and would do as Joy dictated as he didn't want to be left all on his own......poor wee boy.

Bertie now had his ammunition and primed his guns accordingly. So, it was on a hot and dry Wednesday afternoon that Bertie made his offer to purchase the entire business with its current five-year lease and right of renewal for a further five years.

The asking price was $100,000. Bertie's offer was $75,000 which as could be expected was not pleasing to either Leroy or Joy and Leroy began to dig his toes in but was quickly and firmly over ridden by Joy as who knows when another buyer may come their way. Offer accepted. However much to the displeasure of the sellers Bertie was not yet finished and he made it quite clear that from the $75,000 he would deduct the amount of $382.50 cents being the amount they had charged him in board and lodgings since his arrival. It was then that he did thank them for the single can of beer that had come free of charge when they had first met by the pool. Since that memorable event he had been charged for each and everything. Now the price to be paid was $74,617.50 Leroy's face began to turn the color of a ripe strawberry and he managed to splutter out something to the affect that Bertie couldn't do that. What did he mean can't do that, Bertie had done just exactly that? Again, with great reluctance they accepted Bertie's adjusted offer. Leroy although still the color of that ripe strawberry and sweating profusely started to talk about a payment schedule and times to be at the bank the following day. Now it was time for Bertie to play his final card and in all honesty, Bertie had a feeling that this card could well mean that the deal would fall over but fuck it in for a penny in for a pound. Bertie politely advised Leroy to slow down and not get ahead of the situation as there was one final deduction of $1,000 to be made. Bloody hell that really fired up Leroy and he rose out of his chair screaming that what the fuck was that for, at the same time Joy knew they had been fucked and didn't utter a single word but if her looks could kill then Bertie was dead ten times over. Calmly and clearly, Bertie explained that the $1, 000 he would pay to Mir to compensate her for loss of earnings and a monetary apology from them both for her mistreatment during her employment. That certainly put the big bad cat amongst the little feathered Pidgeon's and Leroy was going ballistic telling Bertie to fuck off, to which Bertie replied no problem and headed to his room to pack his bag.

No more than 10 minutes had passed when there was a knock on his door and who should it be but the sweet smiling bitch that was Joy. They would accept the final offer of $73,617.50 cents on the condition that the amount would be paid in full within 7 days. Bertie agreed, and over the next 24 hours purchase agreements were drawn up and thumb printed by all parties and that is simply how Bertie who couldn't do that did indeed do exactly that and became the owner of a guesthouse, bar restaurant and swimming pool complex in the small Cambodian border town of Korrup Kong.

Chapter 4

The sight of Leroy and Joy climbing into the Tuk-tuk that was going to take them the 8 kilometers to the Cambodian Thai border checkpoint was a welcome sight. Mir had started back at work that very morning and it was great to have her back and see her smiling. Bertie, Mir and two other staff members lined up on the footpath outside the restaurant to bid them farewell. As the Tuk-tuk pulled away from the curb all four waved them off and from Bertie it wasn't a wave that wished them a safe journey no it was a wave with two fingers pointing to the sky above and forming an impressive and unmistakable V and Mir could have sworn she heard Bertie call out "Fuck off and don't come back"

Although Mir's spoken English was good it did take considerable time for Bertie to get her to understand why he was giving her $1000.00. Yes, time and patience on Bertie's part. Initially she backed right off as if Bertie was handing her something unlawful and at any minute the police would arrive and Mir's small hands would be locked in rough and heavy iron bracelets and she would spend the rest of her days deep within the confines of the dark and damp local "Monkey House" but eventually all was settled and Mir was back to having a smile on her face. One could possibly say a smile with a hint of added interest.

$1000.00 was a lot of money considering the average monthly wage for someone like Mir was $110.00 so yes here in her little hand was the equivalent of about 9 months' pay.

Time to get this ship back on course and up to speed now that the dirty stagnant bilge water had been pumped out onto a Tuk-tuk bound for the border. What exactly did Bertie have to keep him occupied and out of trouble? Well at least for a little while. In no particular order he had: seven poolside double rooms plus a further three that were adjacent to the pool: one swimming pool measuring 15M x 4M with a consistent depth of 3.6 M : a small but well equipped and functional kitchen: one office come store room: one bar / restaurant with seating capacity for 30 hungry and thirsty diners/drinkers, plus standing room along the bar for those that were capable of standing allowed a possible addition of 6 to 8, depending on just how friendly they were with each other: upstairs accommodation for himself and any lucky lady that may be invited up to spend a few hours of fine company care of mine host after closing time.

In order to keep the cogs of this small enterprise turning smoothly Bertie had a full-time crew of five, plus two others that were required to help with the breakfast rush as this was the busiest time of the day for meals and would kick off at about 0700hrs and run thru till perhaps 1000hrs. The full menu was available throughout opening hours and as Bertie was not one to conform to the normal then on his list of things to do was change the footpath sign promoting "All Day Breakfast" to "Breakfast All Day" mmmmm he did wander if he could run a patent on that.

Once the breakfast crowd had departed on organized local tours or continuing their journeys to places and planets further afield was when Bertie headed to the open market close by. Yes, close by, no further than 100 meters and there he bought a selection of seafood, vegies and fruit. Why? Was he heading to the riverfront to have a late breakfast on his own? Of course not. Have you not by now realized Bertie was a generous person who deep down cared about others and besides it was time for all staff members including himself to get together and go over a few basics. Everyone seated at a table with good food did turn out to be a good idea.

Bertie was well pleased with his selection and the plastic bags full of goodies he presented to Mir who was up to her elbows at the kitchen sink washing dirty breakfast dishes. Could Bertie not see Mir had her hands full so he was politely told "one minute Bertie" Anyway about ten minutes passed before Mir was ready to be advised about the contents of these plastic bags now lined up along the bench. Where had Bertie disappeared to? Was he sulking somewhere as a result of an almost uninterested response to his bringing of fine food?

Oh no, far from it. Bertie was in his comfortable poolside chair. His once piping hot mug of coffee was now far from hot as it sat there untouched but the ashtray on the small bamboo framed glass topped table had adopted two new butts and was preparing for a third. He was at it again and in a barely audible voice he was praising himself for seeing since his arrival prior to her voluntary departure the great possibilities and potential in Mir. Unknowingly she had reinforced his thoughts and feelings when she told him simply "one minute Bertie" Others would have shied away or without thinking delved into the plastic bags with hands unknowingly giving the contents a good showering of dirty dishwater and suds. Bertie just knew that Mir given time, encouragement and help, such attitudes and actions she had previously been denied, that she would then develop and build her own confidence and become an excellent manageress.

It seemed all hands were to the pump converting plastic bags of assorted food into numerous great looking and tasty dishes which were without ceremony placed on several tables that had been pushed together so all could be seated. Small talk, no make that noisy chatter between mouthfuls of one dish or the other bounced between this gathering of all staff members and when after longer than Bertie thought was possible, he at last was able to address them. Mir who was seated to his left naturally took on the job of interpreting to those that could not understand just what Bertie thought was important for them to know and understand. He began with a warm welcome and how pleased he was to have them all as members of his staff, and moved quickly to let them know he would not tolerate stealing in any shape or form but on the other hand if they were experiencing difficulties of any type, they could come and talk with him and he would help them as much as possible to overcome any such problems. He assured them that he would not be pinching their bums or expecting sexual favors of any kind and if any customers should think that they could treat them with disrespect of any nature then just walk away and Bertie would sort out any troublesome types.

They were not to go to any rooms alone with guests so if they had thoughts along those lines of making any extra income then forget it now. If that is what they wanted then he would gladly show them the door and they would probably be more suited to employment at one of several Chicken Farms located on the outskirts of town.

Bloody hell well into chapter four and finally a mention of Chicken Farms.........but that's enough for now.

In finishing he thanked them all for their attendance and let them know he felt confident that if they all worked together then "our establishment" would soon become the best on offer in Korrup Kong.

They all helped clearing away the dishes and Bertie had to be extra quick to fill his plate with one more helping of that delicious concoction of squid, vegetables and pineapple, simply superb. Bertie was very pleased with how things had gone, not forgetting Mir's important role as translator. There was going to be some changes but now wasn't the time to introduce them. Generally, people fear changes especially changes introduced by someone they hardly know, so let's just all get to know each other a little better was Bertie's next step.

Two items on Bertie's must do yesterday list was rewording the 'All day breakfast" sign and make up a new sign, the new sign read;

"WELCOME TO THE RUSTY ANCHOR!!
Here the customer is not always right.
Some of you bring us happiness when you arrive
Some of you bring us great joy when you leave

Which one are you?"

Finding a competent sign writer was a challenge but finally after five frustrating attempts the sign was completed. The day had arrived and with great ceremony and a gathering of all staff that happened to be present Bertie secured the sign on the wall behind the bar which also served as a reception area for the incoming guests. He positioned it in such a way that no one could possibly miss seeing it, so no excuses. Explaining the sign to Mir and staff was indeed another challenge and best understood as the days passed when Bertie had opportunities to demonstrate its purpose with real live guests. Some might say they were cannon fodder. Well, some were and they deserved to be so. Bertie could just as easily tell someone to fuckoff as alternatively he would go to extremes to make good customers feel welcome.

Bertie's simple philosophy was that he started each day at 5.30am and didn't finish some days till near midnight. Each day he began with a full tank of gas / energy and how he used it was up to him.

He was much the happier wee soul if he used it on good customers that respected the staff and understood they were in Cambodia paying about $15.00 per night for a poolside air-conditioned room. Customers that simply got on with enjoying their experience of being in an extremely poor country, after all that's why they came here as adverse to pouncy fuckers that thought they were on the Frogs Riviera treating the staff like slaves and clicking their bony fingers expecting everyone to run after them. Bertie didn't run after these self-important and extremely opinionated dickheads of both sexes and he didn't expect his staff to. He simply walked up to them and told them to pack their bags and fuck off. That's when he usually got told that he couldn't do that as they were his guests, well guess what he just did and if needed to prove he could then he simply shut off the electricity to their room and put on the pretense that he was calling his very good friend in the local police force. Needless to say, they were soon packed and on their way. Bertie was particular and made sure any refunds that may be due were paid as they made their somewhat embarrassed exit passing the smiling staff that simply stood and waved goodbye.

Going to extremes some of you may think. Not at all and let's put it into some sort of perspective and understand that at least 90% of The Rusty Anchor's guests were great people, so the pack your bags fuck off scenarios were few and far between. Yes, a few situations did get a little physical and worth mentioning was an incident that did just that.

Let's just leap ahead for an example, one afternoon about one year after taking ownership Bertie had cause to speak to a couple in their 30's as they were having a heated domestic argument poolside. After being spoken to the cooled down quickly and nothing else was heard, problem solved? Wishful thinking, as at about 7pm they entered the bar and it was obvious they were both off their faces on drugs or booze maybe even both. Whatever, they both decided to reignite their earlier domestic, well Bertie's bar was not the place for such an event and as he made his way towards the offensive couple the male of the species punched his partner full in the face resulting in a bloody mouth and one front tooth hanging precariously from some upper gum tissue. Bertie quickly closed the distance and with his left hand got a strong grip on the hitter's hair and at the same time landed a cupped right hand hard down on his left ear which certainly caused bells to ring in whatever grey matter remained inside and as a bonus he would surely have a perforated eardrum. Bertie was now in full swing and dragged this wretched soul out into the street where he knocked him to the ground and knelt heavily on his neck in order to restrain his somewhat violent struggles to resist.

A small crowd had gathered and two police officers quickly arrived and took control so Bertie did not need to maintain downward pressure for approximately 8 minutes and keep in sync with the latest instructions and live videos that some world news broadcasting stations had been showing repeatably. He was free to return behind his bar and continue with polishing glasses or whatever it was he was doing before being rudely interrupted.

Mir had stepped up to the mark and taken care of the toothless one. Bertie reluctantly allowed her to stay the night but she must be out at first light. It could well be imagined that she had a much more comfortable night than her male sparring partner that would have had the memorable experience of spending the night in a cramped cell and released the next morning but only after paying an exceedingly heavy fine.

Let us go back now, and pick up to when Bertie met some of Korrup Kong's finest. Yes, that's right the police.

He had already been visited by Immigration and Tourism officials so did have his visa, work permit and Tourism License therefore all was in order......thank goodness for that.

It was about midafternoon give an hour or two either way when Mir knocked on his office door and informed him that the police had arrived. It was thru his recently self-made spy hole located in the wall of his office and which gave him a visual over most of the bar and restaurant that he spotted not one, not two but in total eight members of the force who had seated themselves at the long table that served for purposes of Al Fresco dining and was obviously in full view of all that passed by. An obvious ploy by the current visitors enabling the townsfolk to see that those in charge of law and order were doing their job.

Bertie's first thought was how nice for Snow White and her seven dwarfs to come visiting disguised as policemen. Hey one has to look on the funny side. If the truth be known Bertie was quite concerned but even so as he approached the committee, he couldn't help thinking maybe he should take out his pencil and order book and ask them if they would like their eggs fried, scrambled or poached and would that be white or whole meal toast on the side. Restraining himself he kept those thoughts to himself and just simply and politely introduced himself. Snow White was not one for messing about and quickly made it plain that he and his seven dwarfs would kick Bertie out of town if he dealt in either drugs or prostitution from the premises of The Rusty Anchor. Bertie's mind quickly ticked over thinking that those before him had no intention in sharing the hidden and unspoken profits that they made from dare I say it? yep, nah changed my mind as am sure you can figure it out for yourselves.

Bertie assured all present at the long table that he would happily obey the laws of Korrup Kong. His voice intentionally loud enough to include a few locals passing by that had pulled up short feigning interest in perhaps that new crack in the pavement but well within earshot of the current event, they could at best understand Snow White but were not sure what the farang (foreigner) had to say.

Handshakes all around, and off they headed back to the Bat Cave for a late afternoon nap. All is well that ends well......

The main purpose of the second monthly meeting was to let all staff members know that from then on if Bertie wasn't present then they were to take directions from Mir as she was now formally manageress. Bertie had previously talked privately with Mir requesting her acceptance of the promotion. Although initially reluctant Bertie assured her that he knew she was well suited and she finally agreed.

The meeting began with the meal and the incessant chatter that went with it. At last, a chance for Bertie to have a little chatter to all assembled. He had come prepared as he knew that not all would be pleased with news of Mir's promotion. To show his appreciation of their efforts he had delegated each one of the four with a responsibility of their own, thus creating their own importance. With Mir's help he had written in Khmer each job on a separate slip of paper and these he placed inside an unused saucepan, stirred them up with a wooden spoon, and spoke some magic words which created a bit of humor then each staff member in no order reached in and withdrew a single slip and read out what her particular responsibility was. Facial expressions varied and it was then that Bertie told them they could swap around with each other but any swapping had to be done before they went home at the end of today's shift. Tomorrow would be too late. Deadlines had to be set and they had to understand that the job they had was totally theirs's to carry out and see it was completed on time and to a high level. This was also the ideal time for Bertie to explain that if all the work was done, he had no problem with them sitting in the restaurant and watching Khmer TV if no guests were present, but no slacking until all work was carried out.

Bertie had in his younger days worked for bosses that expected you to be doing something all the time. Well, what's the bloody point of picking up a broom and sweeping what you finished sweeping just because the boss walked by. Bertie detested this attitude and no way was he having his staff on tender hooks every time he appeared.

Bertie called a close to the meeting and as the staff made ready to leave, he dealt his final card. Once again with Mir's help, he explained that with their new personal responsibilities they would all receive a small pay increase. This time all the facial expressions were the same, happy smiles all around.

Chapter 5

Ok let's give Bertie a break, don't worry he will still be there when we return as Mir presented him with a list of maintenance chores that need to be addressed.

We will move on and do a little geography just to get a basic idea of where Bertie has ended up. There is no need for you to stress out as there is no requirement for either a written or oral exam to be undertaken upon conclusion.

Korrup Kong is approximately 300k's by road to the SW of Cambodia's capital Phnom Penh and about 8k's from the Cambodian Thai border. It was built on the banks of the Korrup river well before I can remember. Now ain't that a coincidence sharing the same first name but because the river was there first then it rightfully retains bragging rights. Population? I have no idea as where does the province start and where does it end. Those people that were here last week have now moved on. Due into town at about lunch time is a truck carrying 20 to 30 men women and children, some will find work and stay on where others will return to the farming district that they came from, so even with the aid of an abacus I could not tell you.

Bertie's guesthouse now renamed "The Rusty Anchor" as its former name "Leroy's House" had disappeared along with its previous owners was situated on the main street. The main street was the 3rd street back from the river front. There were no traffic lights or much in the way of rules of the road and even at the roundabout traffic for the most part ran smoothly with just the odd accident from time to time. Exiting the roundabout to the right would take you to the river front. Take a left and you would immediately be on Chicken Farm Road. Once again, the mention of the Chicken Farm arises and in due course we will discuss the pros and cons of this area, but not now.

Five k's downstream and in a southerly direction is the river mouth and there it enters the Gulf of Thailand. About 2k's in the same direction and on the same side of the river built on timber piles and extending over the river is the Muslim fishing village. The village population is highly congested and comprises predominantly of Muslims and fish, well what would you expect to find in a Muslim fishing village? A long-necked Giraffe with pink spots and pimples on its arse??

At the northern end of the main township a very long bridge has been built over the river which since its opening has reduced travel time up to the border check point before crossing into Thailand. Yes, a very long bridge 1.8k's long to be exact but it had to be that long because the first one they built was not long enough.

Not long enough? Yes, that's what I said. The whole town gathered for the opening ceremony of the first bridge. The acting governor cut the ribbon but before he could return to the motorcade numbering perhaps a dozen cars of varying ages and in states of disrepair that would transport him and selected town dignitaries across the pride of the town two overly eager Tuk-tuk *drivers drove onto and along the bridge. They were going at full speed with flags and different colored balloons flying from their flimsy wire aerials then suddenly they reached the end and over into the fast-flowing river they went and with two large splashes they disappeared never to be seen again. As I said earlier the first bridge that was built just wasn't long enough and what was meant to be a day of pomp and ceremony turned into a day of deep grief and even deeper disappointment. A wasted trip for those that had travelled down from Phnom Penh for the big occasion.*

Who was responsible for this major hiccup? The Chinese bridge building company "Wecanspan Ltd" blamed the town planners and they in turn blamed "Wecanspan Ltd". The blame bounced back and forth over several months and still Korrup Kong remained without its bridge. Oh, not all was lost as the bridge that wasn't long enough became a popular place to go fishing. New parents could stroll along pushing their newborns in a variety of home-built prams. As the sun set in the West young lovers could walk its length whispering sweet nothings to each other. Mind you none of that happened until a secure safety barrier had been erected at the bridges abrupt end. Korrup Kong could not afford to lose any more of its citizens especially Tuk-tuk drivers as good honest ones were hard to find.

The Governor although not the brightest bulb in the chandelier but certainly with the townsfolks wellbeing at heart had to do something. It was after days of deep thought and nights spent consulting with the stars above, he finally had a solution. He would build a new bridge but this time it would reach the far side of the river. A brilliant idea and his house staff congratulated him and some even slapped him gently on his back. It was easy to see now why he was the Governor; he really was the man. A true legend in the making.

He arranged a meeting between the head of town planning and the Chinese civil engineer representing "Wecanspan Ltd" He asked them to put their differences behind them and work together to create and construct this bridge that would go the distance in fact all the way to the other side of the Korrup river, after all is that not what bridges are designed and built for? Finally, after a somewhat heated session of blame being passed back and forth for a faulty first attempt to cross the river both parties came to an agreement that they would work together and see this incredible feat of engineering and construction techniques result in a workable and practical bridge. Glasses of whiskey were raised and downed and handshakes all around.

Eyewitnesses to this agreement would have noticed that the head of town planning quickly checked to see all fingers still remained on the hand he had used to shake the hand of the Chinaman.

The combined effort was a great success. It took several years but finally the bridge was opened and firm friendships grew between the town planners and "Wecanspan Ltd" The Governor promised that if any further bridges were to be built then his Chinese friends would get first option and completely to his surprise several days later a plain brown envelope bulging at its seams was delivered to his private dwellings. This envelope the Governor quickly squirreled away beneath his single straw mattress to *save for a rainy day or perhaps he would take it on his next trip to the capitol city Phnom Penh. There he could put it to good use in his pursuit of the delights that Hostess girls would eagerly share in exchange for some of the contents of that plain brown envelope.*

Now you are all orientated and filled your camera with pictures of both bridges lets head back to The Rusty Anchor and see if Bertie has finished his chores.

Oh, look there he is poolside in his comfy chair beside the potted fern. The poor guy looks worn out but showing definite signs of life as he lifts and drinks from his can of beer, perhaps his 5th can if those empties under his chair are his.

Chapter 6

Following the allocation of staff duties, the atmosphere improved immensely. All of a sudden, they found they had a defined purpose, they had responsibilities and each in their own way was determined to be the best. Those that initially had resented Mir's promotion now looked to her for help and guidance, which Mir happily provided. No time now for petty arguments and or bitching, oh and Mr. Bertie, oops he doesn't like that as he much prefers just good and simple Bertie well, he is quite a funny fellow and he pitches in where he can. However, his attempts in the kitchen were quickly blocked as anything he cooked Mir simply tasted, and dismissed with,

"No good sour Bertie"

If Bertie had boiled up a kg of sugar the response would have been the same. He simply could not win on that one and he was happy to accept a comical banishment from the kitchen as he was getting so much enjoyment in seeing Mir grow and develop. Amongst her peers and villagers, she was now referred to as, 'oh that's Mir she is the Manageress of The Rusty Anchor"

The Rusty Anchor was trading well above what he had predicted and Bertie had found time to start making friends with both locals and expats. Actually, acquaintances were a term that better describes his relationships with the expats whom had found themselves a Khmer lady friend and rented houses up on stilts. Upstairs was for living and downstairs was converted to a bar of sorts. All that was needed was a few cane chairs, a flat screen TV, some music and alcohol. Perhaps if the lady was enterprising then she may put on a couple of simple rice dishes, extra spicey rice dishes to encourage consumption of cold beer. Oh, and let's not forget the communal dog end that was frequently passed around and puffed on by those present. They really did not cause any harm and I am sure Snow White and his seven dwarfs never went short of tea money. Bertie had to admit that he made his monthly contribution as each day "Happy" would call by to pick up a copy of the guest's registrar and on the 20th of each month he would also pick up a $5.00 note which as if by sleight of hand would disappear into the top pocket of his freshly laundered and ironed tunic. Happy was a pretty good guy and made sure that as long as the $5.00 kept coming then no hassles from his partners in the force, (bloody hell nearly wrote crime) would Bertie have to endure. Yes, Happy was worth his monthly stipend of $5.00

Bertie decided that he was going to clad one wall of the bar with split bamboo. After making a few inquiries re procurement of said bamboo he was informed that it would have to be brought down the river by boat at night time as the police would be sleeping. Once it reached the town it was then ok for it to be delivered during daylight hours with no problems. Are you a bit confused? Well Bertie was and he certainly asked a few questions but finally with great doubt and apprehension he agreed. A date was set for a dark and moonless night and sure enough down the river and passing under two bridges came a small and grossly overloaded boat with Bertie's bamboo. At about 10am the following morning a motor bike towing a small but grossly overloaded cart transporting Bertie's bamboo pulled up outside The Rusty Anchor. Bertie, still not convinced that this was the way some things happened quickly formed his staff into a chain gang and got the possibly incriminating cargo stowed inside and out of sight......fuck it was that green the birds were still in it. Mir helped calm his nerves by making him a coffee heavily laced with Rum and as if nothing untoward had happened The Rusty Anchor continued with its normal activities.

Stage one of the bamboo sagas had been completed and stage two began several weeks later once the birds had packed up their nests and left for more promising surrounds. Armed with his power saw and electric drill Bertie began cladding the nominated wall, dreading the appearance of Happy on his daily visit. Happy never missed a day and this day was no different. With great importance he strode into the bar, ran his hand over some of the bamboo already secured in place, looked Bertie straight in the eye and with a wry smile simply said,

"This looks good, nice bamboo Bertie"

He then collected the guest's registration form and bid Bertie a nice day. Yep, Happy was an ok guy and Bertie soon had one wall of his bar clad in nice bamboo and yes it did look good.

Fathers and mothers, brothers and sisters had heard from Bertie's staff that he treated them well and with respect so slowly and surely, he was being accepted throughout the community. It was not uncommon for him to be invited to functions of varying types, predominantly weddings and at many of these functions he was introduced to single women also of varying types but being single was one feature they all had in common. Well one doesn't have to have to be Sherlock Holmes to understand the reason for invites to some of the functions.

Tuk-tuk drivers and taxi drivers, a mixed bunch of scallywags and scam artists if ever a group of such dubious reputations existed. Being fair at the end of the day they were all trying to make a living and most of them were just a little bit dishonest but of course there were a few that it was extremely wise to steer well clear of.

The foreigner arriving at the border checkpoint immediately came under fire and some of those arriving had somewhere whilst travelling on life's journey lost any plain common sense, were so naïve and lacked even a small amount of street smarts despite obviously having spent time in neighboring Thailand that they deserved to fall prey to the jackals that waited in plain view in and around the Immigration Office.

If they managed to dodge the phony Dr in his white smock coat and wearing a stethoscope like perhaps some ornate necklace claiming that all visitors' temperatures had to be taken, then it was usually Immigration officials that took the first bite by charging inflated visa prices.

Phew!! But far from over as plenty more to come. If you had decided to travel the 8 k's to the township by taxi, then the moment you closed the taxi door the driver would begin to try and persuade you that there was absolutely nothing to do in Korrup Kong and it was a dangerous town, much better if he took you thru to Sihanoukville with its beautiful beaches etc. etc. Much better for who? Well obviously, the taxi driver as he would then pick up a fare of close to $100.00 as compared to the original destination which would be about $10.00 Decisions, decisions and the driver seems like a nice guy, he even knows of a really good safe guesthouse right by the beach in Sihanoukville..................mmmmmm

However, after four or five hours in a cramped minivan, perhaps it would be nicer to enjoy the openness of a Tuk-tuk for the short run to the town and the driver knows a great place to change some Thai baht into Cambodian riel. Well of course he does, a great place for him to get a backhander and the foreigner to get an absolutely piss poor exchange rate.

You say, common sense is all that is required to avoid such scams and yes you are correct. Then why does it happen and happen it does. Bertie knows only too well as he has listened repeatedly to tales of woe from distraught, confused and sometimes those in tears about their costly misadventures.

Let's look a little deeper into associating with or without these fine upstanding carriers of the human populace. Fortunately, Bertie did befriend two brothers, Bart and Harry whom each had their own Tuk-tuk's and agreed that for the fee of $5.00 each (that magic number again) per month they would attach a sign advertising The Rusty Anchor to their fine chariots. Of course, Bertie had to foot the bill for the manufacture of these signs. No such thing as a free lunch especially in Korrup Kong. As per normal Bertie had one more card to play and he required either Bart or Harry to meet at the border customers that had made prior bookings to stay at The Rusty Anchor. This was met with some animosity by other drivers as they did run a rostered system as to whose day it was to be at the border or bus station. So, a little sorting out had to be done by Bart and Harry, not really Bertie's problem and it did make a more comfortable arrival to Korrup Kong for guests who had wisely decided to book ahead and stay at The Rusty Anchor.

Hey, hey as we all know only too well every coin has two sides. There was a very loose understanding that if a driver bought a guest to a guesthouse, then the guesthouse would pay them $1.00 Bertie disagreed with this and would not pay if the guests had pre-booked or if they had specifically asked to be taken to The Rusty Anchor. Alternatively, if the driver upon being asked to recommend a guesthouse had indeed recommended The Rusty Anchor, then Bertie was only too happy to pay the $1.00 Simple enough one would think but not that simple and confusion raised its ugly head. Bertie did not like confusion so he called a meeting of the senior drivers and explained how he intended to operate regardless of any previous loose understanding. To conclude he added that all drivers would be contacted and given first option if and when the guests that they delivered required further means of transport. The reaction was mixed to say the least some thought it was fine, but others became quite angry and spoke out so all could hear that they would never bring a guest to his place. Oh well one can't win them all, but it sure is good fun trying.

Bertie cannot recall how many times he died in the years that followed, his death usually a result of a motorcycle accident only just the day before, or perhaps he had just up and left, or was imprisoned because he was caught stealing mangoes from the open market, and any one of a dozen other reasons why The Rusty Anchor was no longer open. These barefaced lies offered to tourists by the disgruntled drivers were quickly followed with,

"No problem I take you to a nice hotel "

Oh, for sure some believed these tales of remarkable and convenient events, so were then surprised when taking a stroll around the small town after settling into some less comfortable accommodation at an inflated price that they came across The Rusty Anchor doors open and operating on all six cylinders.

Regular returning guests, usually expats from Thailand doing a visa run would not believe such bullshit and demand to be taken to The Rusty Anchor which really did fire up the drivers as it was either that or no fare at all.

It was indeed fortunate that Bertie had befriended Bart & Harry, combined with his hard-earned popularity amongst the townsfolk due to the way he treated and respected his staff that probably saved Bertie from an early and untimely termination of life. Some lives could be easily and cheaply bought in the small border town of Korrup Kong.

Chapter 7

Several meters from The Rusty Anchor was the second roundabout on the town's main street and hanging a turn to the left upon reaching this point would put travelers, yes male and female directly onto Chicken Farm Road. Continuing on this road for a further 2 k's and they would find themselves in a rural setting and clustered in close proximity of each other a variation of different dwellings all offering slightly different versions of the same activities.

The tentacles of a worldwide fast-food chain had not yet reached Korrup Kong therefore as often as not the area would be referred to as KFC, usually by drunkards unable to connect their brain with their raspy and indistinguishable vocal systems making it impossible for them to put together the local title of Chicken Farm.

Bertie had often ridden his trustee steed thru the area, returning waves where he felt it was appropriate, never stopping to buy but on occasions passing the time of day with Henny. Bertie and Henny had what could for all intents and purposes be called a love hate relationship. Their meetings were brief and usually just covered the latest town gossip. Bertie knew he could recommend Henny's chicks to some of his guests and in return there were no problems created for his guests which often resulted in problems for Bertie. Trustee steed? No, you are wrong as it was neither a water buffalo or a long-eared donkey trying to eat a carrot on the end of a stick. Bertie's trustee steed was a Taiwanese Sym Wolf motor bike boasting 150cc of pure raw power with a manual four speed gear box. The best vehicle of any kind that Bertie had ever owned.

The main players governing the Chicken Farm complex was the twin sister and brother team of Henny and Rooster. Henny was the older of the two and if anyone had taken note of the old plastic clock hanging above the straw bed in the corrugated iron shed that served as a delivery room then Henny was only out and thru the gates 45 seconds before Rooster was held hanging by his ankles and given a good slapping.

They ran their own establishments which were directly opposite each other on the main dusty road that wound its way thru the assortment of available and varied entertainment venues.

There was no mistaking these two fine places as each had a roadside sign that even for the drunkard it was impossible to miss,

Henny's sign read;

COCKADOODLEDO
Cold Beers and Chicks!!

Rooster's sign read;

ANYCOCKWILLDO
Cold Beers and Dicks!!

During the day these signs welcomed the shade from the overhead Mango trees and by night danced to the multi colored flickering lights attached to their perimeters.

No one that had met Henny and Rooster would argue against the obvious, Henny was the brains and Rooster was the muscle and there was no mistaking the pecking order. It was Henny that had decided they should both have a separate establishment and Rooster didn't offer much opposition when it was his place that Henny decided would offer a wider range of activities and that she would run the coop of normality. When asked why it was that way, not often but still sometimes asked she would simply reply;

"We operate the world's oldest profession and we have spread our wings to encompass and to provide for all those that care to grace our humble dwellings with their presence and Rooster just happens to be better equipped to handle some of the less regular and sometimes volatile requests"

Henny ran a brood of chicks that presented a fine and colorful display of varying plumage. They were pretty, friendly and only those that could prove they were over 18 years old and under 35 were ever offered nesting rights behind the mesh fence that encompassed Cockadoodledo. They were not locals but from other provinces further to the north and from time-to-time Henny would introduce an international flavor and source a couple of bantams from across the Vietnamese border. An extended family member but an old boiler that she was made up the afterguard and it was her job to settle any differences or squabbles that arose within the brood resulting mainly in peaceful and tranquil surrounds.

Therefore, if one was looking for some limited conversation, lots of fun, laughter perhaps a game of cards and drinks in the small but well-kept beer garden followed by a romp and scratch in the hay then Cockadoodledo ticked all the boxes.

Alternatively, Anycockwilldo directly across the road and located on what was known as the dark side also provided entertainment for sure. However, there was no well-kept beer garden or outside seating of any type and black shadows from low slung roof lines overgrown with vines and other vegetation danced without care or consideration across the poorly cobbled and rubbish strewn path that led to the front entrance.

Slouching either side of the cracked and warped timber door there would always be two of Roosters robust but scruffy security Cockerels who found great pleasure in roughly frisking any guest and seemed to linger longer on those of the fairer sex. Oh yes here at Anycockwilldo all perversions and fantasies were available, well almost any. Upon the insistence from Henny, Rooster also kept his mixed ménage to those over the age of 18 but held no limit to upper age so did indeed have several old boilers, at certain times of the night demand would be such that they would often be run off their spindly ancient claws, creating I have been told not a pretty sight.

If one was looking for beauty then go no further than Cockadoodledo. If your sexual tendencies and or persuasions drew you to perhaps search for a cock in a frock, or 15 minutes of furious scissoring followed by an additional 15 minutes of damaging dildos, maybe a severe whipping incorporating partial strangulation was your preferred specialty or numerous alternatives and you found yourself within the musky poorly lit confines of Anycockwilldo then there you would find your desires and fantasies fulfilled. These services understandably demanded a higher-than-normal price due to the surcharge on the standard amount of monthly tea money that each and every chicken house shelled out. Bloody hell nearly forgot but as sure as eggs are eggs if indeed you did damage any property, dildo's do spring to mind then make no mistake you would pay at an inflated price the full cost of replacements. No!! doesn't matter if it wasn't your fault as the simple reasoning is if you were not there then it would not have happened so how can it be anyone else's.

Bertie and Rooster steered well clear of each other. They had in the not-too-distant past come extremely close to trading blows and if it had not been for Henny's intervention then blood and feathers would have flown in all directions including some that would have landed in the stagnant water bowl located just to the left of the back entrance to Anycockwilldo where this unpleasant event transpired. The reason for the altercation was not known except perhaps to the antagonists but everyone did know that Bertie could be an exceedingly stubborn, obstinate being and wasn't shy of sorting things with a bit of physical activity if the situation required such an additional ingredient. Everyone also knew that Rooster had a huge dent in his feathers and had carried that dent for most of his life, most certainly all of his adult life. This dent had grown over the years and was primarily caused by everyone on meeting Rooster and finding out that he had a twin sister had without exception all asked the same question;

"Who arrived first and by how much time?"

No one ever asked as to who came second and it clouded Rooster's outlook on life that no one really cared about who came second. Almost a case of a fine effort but no cigar. Life can be oh so very cruel… and deep-down Rooster would one day show the world well at the very least the neighboring provinces that he demanded and deserved respect even I dare say if the demise of Henny was necessary.

In close proximity there were several other establishments that operated with what one may say a looser set of rules and cheaper prices. It was some of these that could and did perhaps unintentionally cause a few problems for Bertie as combined with guests that thought they knew it all was a recipe for just a bit of unpleasantness.

A typical scenario began with a guest asking Bertie if it was ok to bring back a chick for the night. No problem with that as rooms were for maximum of two adults and Bertie would suggest that for an all-night romance it was best, they find a chick at the Cockadoodledo. He went on to explain in simple sentences that chicks from other hen houses would after you paid $20.00 to the mother hen gladly accompany you back to your room, turn on the TV, sit on your bed and within a few minutes surprise surprise!!! their phone would ring. A quick conversation in Khmer would transpire and then an apology explaining that big problem at her hen house and she must go back immediately. It just so happened that the Tuk-tuk driver they had just used was still outside and no you won't be welcome as she must return alone.................. So down $20.00 plus, and no night of romance with a happy ending and promises of seeing each other again the following evening. Of course, those that thought they knew better just did not pay heed to Bertie's suggestions and they paid the price. The Tuk-tuk driver was also in on the scam for was he not the same one that had persuaded with very little effort that gullible dickhead to just try that particular hen house on the ride out? Of course, it fucking well was. Some people are so blind in one eye that they just can't see out of the other and go thru life with the lights out.

Next morning when Bertie asked the now not so cocky guest how did his night go, the reply would always begin with

"You would never guess what happened to me last night"

Fuck Bertie wished he had a $1.00 for every time he had heard that and I am sure the slightly intelligent ones amongst you can guess exactly what did transpire so I won't waste your time by going thru the scenario again!!!!

There was a multitude of various and similar cases that bounced back and forth between The Rusty Anchor and its sparring partners located up the dusty road, yes that dusty road referred to by all simply as Chicken Farm Road and was printed out as such on tourist and backpackers fold up maps, even possibly on a satellite map accessible on some of those new smart phones which were gaining popularity.

One such event that was a little different and certainly worth a mention. It began at about 5.30 one morning when Bertie was passing the pool on his way to his office. Seated on the edge of the pool with their feet in the water were three chicks and by the condition of their feathers were definitely not any of Henny's brood. Damn security at the front door had probably fallen asleep or what was more likely is one of the chicks seated on the pools edge would have given the guard's manhood a bit of a stroking in return for an unchallenged entry. Good security guys were as common as good hen's teeth and saying that in this neck of the woods could not be a better illustration that finding good reliable staff was indeed a challenge. When asked what they were doing they chirped in unison that they were waiting for their friend and all three pointed to the door of room number two. In reply Bertie picked up a nearby broom and with a bit of effort shooed them from their poolside nest down the path and out the door past the now empty chair normally used to comfort the fat lazy arse of the excuse for security. Yep, he had simply run off and nothing unusual in that trait of behavior, oh well Bertie wandered, will the next one be any better.

The breakfast rush had finished and from his office Bertie could hear the excessive revving of motor scooter engines which almost certainly emanated from the front entrance. Bit of a surprise he did see when he ventured out as Mir and three staff members had formed a human barricade across the entrance. Mir was standing toe to toe with a much larger member of the chook family and a verbal sparring match was taking place all in Khmer so none of it could Bertie understand but it was obvious Mir wasn't inviting her opposite to join her in a cup of tea and a slice of cake. The enemy's army numbering seven meanwhile was keeping up a constant and incessant revving of their scooter engines in a very weak and poor attempt at intimidation. Fuck in his younger day back in NZ Bertie had faced off against biker gangs that were made up of huge bikers and huge motor bikes so this all seemed a bit like a party at the local kindergarten.

Turning on his diplomatic charm Bertie managed to find out that the raiding party had come to collect not one but two members of their feathered gang that were currently in room two. It was then that he did recognize one as being one of the three he had got rid of earlier that day.

Bertie's diplomatic charm quickly disappeared and instructing Mir to hold the fort he made his way to room number two. Bursting thru the closed but carelessly unlocked door he found yes, the two hens plus their benefactor strewn out on the bed in a drunk and or drugged condition. Hastily and with considerable effort he got the hens back into their feathers and out on to the street and to their waiting comrades. With more excessive revving of engines they departed, hung a left turn at the roundabout and headed off up Chicken Farm Road.

Part one of the problem sorted but more to come. By the time he returned to room number two its occupier had reached some low level of consciousness a level that allowed him to argue his case with Bertie......YEP here it comes that scenario when Bertie simply tells him he has got 15 minutes to pack his bags and fuck off, oh and don't forget to pick up your deposit from the front desk on your way out. Of course, Bertie pays no such deposit until he has checked the vacated room for any sign of willful damage or any other reason, that he may choose not to pay any refund and those reasons can be wide and varied.

The dust settles and Bertie thanks his staff but warns them against placing themselves in any path of possible danger in the future. Mir as manageress simply lets Bertie know that it was no problem and that all the village girls would band together, if necessary, as none of them liked the hens that come and go from other provinces and during their stay do sometimes lead some of the village boys and men along crooked paths and she simply finishes by saying;

"You know what I mean Bertie"

Chapter 8

Despite a few ups and downs Bertie was enjoying life running The Rusty Anchor. Yep, life really was pretty good, oh for sure very long hours and it was day after day, week after week which became month after month. A dramatic change from when he worked at sea where he would do six weeks on board ship then have six weeks holiday. Every two weeks whether he be at work or on holiday normally chasing his tail around Thailand his wages would continue to be paid.

The best times of the day were two in number. The first began at 0530hrs when armed with a mug of coffee he had himself constructed with that being one of the rare occasions he would dare venture into Mir's galley, plus more often than not a new pack of cigarettes he would be seated at his office desk going over the previous day's trading. Always happy when the incoming revenue exceeded the outgoings which was not always the case especially on days when water, electricity and wages were paid out. The end of month tallies thankfully always showed the reality of just how his boat was floating and indeed month by month the freeboard was increasing and his sails / sales caught and fully utilized every breath of wind although the seas were sometimes rough and wild. With the top priority taken care of he would then study the sales of various meals and drinks. Which were the top sellers? Which were slow to move and did that price adjustment on certain lines increase or decrease sales? He was continually experimenting with different points of sale and found it all of great interest. What a boring lazy life those guys down in Sihanoukville must lead he often mused to himself. At exactly 0630hrs he would here the unlocking of padlocks and the sliding open of the steel concertina doors that separated the restaurant from the Al fresco dining area and street beyond. Mir had arrived and he would respond to her happy;

"Good morning, Bertie" with an answer much the same and so the day would begin in earnest.

Closing time could be anytime and sometimes he wouldn't pull those concertina doors closed till well after midnight. Mir had finished at her usual time of 1630hrs as he never worked his staff more than 10 hours per day which was slightly less than the normal 12-hour days that most employees were required to work.

Now with the doors closed this became Bertie's very own time. Time to turn on some music and the lights down low. More often than not Leonard Cohens "First We Take Manhattan" would be the starter. A mixed selection which varied from night to night of alcoholic beverages from the top shelf would find their way in to a pint-sized glass, some coke NO not the white powder but the black fizzy stuff, a lump or two of ice would follow and with the help of the wide end of an imitation ivory chopstick Bertie would slowly stir and never shake tonight's cocktail of choice. Within a short period of time the alcohol kicked in, the end of his cigarette glowed a deep red, Leonard was singing all the right words and Bertie was at peace with himself, charging up his batteries for the day to follow. On occasions when it wasn't only his own solitude that he sought then he would set up camp and sip on his medicine in the outside area watching the prowling cats silently and ghostlike as they patrolled their very own patch of the main street. Perhaps like him they were seeking out their very own reason to exist.

The Rusty Anchor's list of house guests ranging from first timers to repeaters was to say at the least a very colorful assortment of the human race. There were those that waved the RUO (Rescue-U Organization) banner proclaiming they were on a crusade to save the poor and impoverished people of Cambodia. Some were genuine, really cared, carried out and achieved some great results which included helping Cambodians improve living standards for themselves and their families. Others noticeably the younger ones, barely out of their nappies / diapers as Bertie would describe them had such high opinions of themselves that their intended stay in the poolside rooms were on more than one occasion cut short. Most of that lot would journey down from Phnom Penh for a few days holiday and some bright prick or prickess amongst them came up with the idea that one of their merry bands would rent a room at The Rusty Anchor and the rest would find cheaper beds elsewhere in the town then at a given time they would all converge poolside. Well, let me tell you in no uncertain manner

Bertie very quickly put a sudden stop to that and a few noses were put out of joint.

"Bloody hell how dare that old bloke Bertie tell us saviors of humanity to piss off" but he did just that and he added don't bloody well come back. The word quickly spread as indeed Bertie had hoped it would and the genuine guests with rooms around the pool found that serenity and tranquility once again ruled.

One of Bertie's biggest hurdles was not being able to speak and understand the Khmer language. He just wasn't one for speaking any other than good old English. It irked him, it worried him and if that wasn't enough it also bothered him especially as his staff tried very hard and with varied amounts of success did come to grips with speaking English. Mir had tried to help him, bless her little cotton socks but given up trying in desperation and frustration as even the simplest of phrases seemed well beyond his grasp and must have asked herself a hundred times "What is wrong with that man?"

Bertie did desperately want to learn the language and sought out tuition from a teacher of high repute. Under this tutor's instructions and examples, he attended his one-on-one classes twice a week. He found it extremely tough going and unknown to him the tutor was finding it even tougher and thoughts of failure were playing hard on his mind, so much so that his wife had mentioned in a whispered voice to several of her close friends that following each lesson her husband would rush home and hit the whiskey bottle. Yes, the whiskey bottle that was normally saved for special events and religious holidays. Why it was only the previous week that the shop assistant had commented to the shop's owner,

"That's the fourth bottle he has bought this month"

When each lesson was finished Bertie then upon his trustee steed would race back to try out his latest learnings upon the patient ear of Mir, repeating each word over and over again as he sped hopefully at last to show how clever he was.

"Mir listen to this" and hardly waiting he would burble forth this latest creation. That same puzzled look would cloud Mir's face and she would simply say,

"What you say Bertie" of course now his breathing had sort of returned to normal, he would try again but with no success and then as if to accept defeat he would say it all in good old English to which Mir would reply with a smile,

"No, Bertie this is how you say it in Khmer"

Wounded but not down and out Bertie persevered with his lessons, then perhaps after 6 or was it 10 weeks? who cares? the tutor as politely as possible suggested that maybe learning to speak Khmer was simply just something Bertie wasn't meant to do. Bertie reluctantly agreed and returned to face Mir and staff members with the disappointing news. In truth the only one disappointed was Bertie as the whiskey bottle at the tutor's house went back to its place in the back corner of the cupboard and only appeared on special events or religious holidays and Mir and staff breathed a joint sigh of relief as no further burbles from an excited Bertie did, they have to try and comprehend.

Al had become a regular guest at The Rusty Anchor and a lighthearted friendship had developed between

Bertie and Al. When he wasn't travelling around Asia Al could be found in his native home of Arizona, USA. Al Anderson was half American Indian and half white fella. He never showed any preference to either half and really could not have cared if hovering on the fringes there was another half of some other race or religion just waiting to become part of Al. His philosophy was simple and as he put it everyone is an individual and should be judged on his or her actions and reasons for such actions, nothing more nothing less, so very simple. Yes, when one thinks about it then one will find it does take into account those that are not so fortunate and may suffer from some physical or mental disability. Al had done several tours of Vietnam as an Infantryman during the troubled years of the Vietnam war and he and some of his surviving buddies had formed a Motorcycle Gang / Club known as "The Legends". A small circle as not too many had returned home but a tight group of mates that enjoyed each other's company and as he told Bertie;

"We are all legends in our own mind and constantly take the piss out of each other"

Al respected all the staff and they in return always looked forward to having him as a guest. He wasn't an early riser as I think his night time activities kept him busy into the early hours of the morning. More often than not at around 10am one of Henny's broods would be seen attempting to make a discreet exit, but not many escaped the watchful eye of Mir who at the first chance would with good humor chastise Al as to his night times activities.

Old Ben was another popular and regular guest whom the staff doted over. Yes, Ben's health had seen better years and he got about at a slow pace with the help of his trusted walking stick but always with a warm smile upon his weathered and wrinkled countenance. He was usually first in for breakfast as he wanted to miss the main rush. A bit of peace and quiet he required as he sipped from his mug of tea and patiently and with shaking of hand spread his toast first with butter then followed with strawberry jam. Ben was a definite favorite of Mir's as it was Mir that asked Bertie if she could double up on the amount of strawberry jam that was usually supplied with the two slices of toast. Bertie was in full agreeance with this gesture of Mir's, and so it was that Ben would have a mug of tea, two slices of toast and jam jam!!!

Ben resided in Pattaya, Thailand and sadly was not in the financial position to get a retirement visa so was destined to make visa runs into Cambodia. He would stay for several days and then head on back over the border. It was most likely that Al and Ben had got to know each other during the afternoon whilst poolside and they became inseparable, well to a certain extent as Ben turned in early and his former youth that may possibly have persuaded him to accompany Al on one of his visits to Cockadoodledo had some time ago got up and left him. Ben had served as a British Paratrooper during the 2nd World War and they enjoyed afternoons chatting and sharing life's experiences by the pool with a cold beer or on some occasions could be seen setting off on a slow walk down to the riverfront. A walk that Ben would take only if Al was with him. Ben would have his main meal in the late afternoon and then retire. A special off the menu meal of selected salads and boiled potatoes that Mir would prepare with care for him and only him.

On the morning of his departure Bertie would present Ben with his bill, a largely discounted bill for his room. There was nothing wrong with Ben's eyesight and he would question why there were no charges for food and drink to which Bertie would reply;

"What food and drink, to the best of my knowledge you had none?"

"Oh ok, thank you but next time I will get you" would be Bens reply.

This scene played out each and every time that Ben came to visit and then suddenly the visits stopped. Several months passed before thru the grapevine Bertie heard what he had for some time expected. Yes, Ben had passed away one afternoon whilst having a sleep on an orange canvas and bamboo framed recliner chair on Pattaya's main beach. According to those that found Ben they say his hands were neatly folded in his lap and protected beneath those hands complete with regimental badge was his tattered and treasured maroon beret which to those that knew Ben sent the simple message that he was "Utrinque Paratus" (Latin) "Ready for Anything" which was the highly respected motto of The British Parachute Regiment.

Everyone was saddened by the news and Mir in particular found it hard. Bertie sent an email to Al and life continued but toast and strawberry jam was a constant reminder of one of the good old guys that were sadly becoming fewer and fewer.

Chapter 9

Bertie had a few, no make that several because several is more than a few but less than many pet hates or shall we soften hates to dislikes? I guess it kind of leans to what crime it is that's being committed and by whom. Bertie extended a huge tolerance to older people and also those with some type of disability either mentally or physically. His tolerance to young people that believed the world owed them a living and showed no consideration to others, well let's just say for practical reasons and to avoid any possible confusion was simply zero.

Therefore, it stands to reason and simple understanding that when young customers plonk themselves down at a table and order a small diet coke or similar, hey no problem so far everything is cool but then they have to fuck it up and without asking they plug their phone or other mobile accessory into the nearest power outlet. Give them credit they are masters at making that drink last for an eternity, Bertie only wished he could do the same with a can of beer.

You remember Al? you should do as you just met him in Chapter 7. He told Bertie on several occasions that he loved being present to watch the following scenario unfold.

Finally, that suck on the straw that heralded at last the empty can and within the next 30 minutes perhaps it will be time to pay the bill and move on. A glance at the bill then a further glance at the menu to check the price of that coke and a confused customer would call Bertie's attention to an overcharge and obvious mistake. Politely Bertie assures the customer there is no overcharge and points out $1.00 for the coke and 50 cents for the electricity so you see no mistake;

"But, but!! I didn't know I had to pay for the electricity" came the whining reply

"You would have if you had the manners to ask and if you had asked then there would have been no charge for the electricity so pay up your inconsiderate excuse for a human and next time maybe you will realize the world doesn't revolve around only you" would be Bertie's standard reply depending on the mood he was in. More often than not a few choice words were added just to add some extra substance to his "don't fuck with me" message.

Of course, a few stood their ground but quickly caved in when Bertie reached for his phone to call his imaginary friend in the local police force.........Another satisfied customer leaves The Rusty Anchor never to return again and of course their departing shot would be something along the lines of;

"I will put this out on the internet and tell everyone"

"But you won't be using my electricity, so piss off" Bertie would reply.

If Al was there, he would clap and request an encore.

Probably a good time to point out that due to the town's proximity to the border then three currencies were in common use and probably in popularity as I list them; $USD, Thai Baht then finally Cambodian Riel. Moving further inland and away from the border the Thai Baht almost disappears but the $USD remained the most common. A cautionary note here is that counterfeit $'s especially in the higher nominations were in circulation and also traders were reluctant to accept any notes that had the tinniest of rips or tears in them no matter how genuine they may be. Oh, so now all of a sudden you are checking your $'s for any damage or possible discrepancies, hope it's not too late.

A constant source of trade came to The Rusty Anchor from Thailand, much of it was repetitive and such was the relationship Bertie had with two separate biker gangs, The JUGGLERS MC and The HENCHMEN MC. They would come at different times and both gangs were always welcome due to the fact that they were great guys and gals and treated the staff with respect, plus they spent big and did not come up short on tips for the staff so everyone looked forward to the roar of their Harleys as they turned into the main street and parked up outside just after midday. Clad in leathers and denims their gang patches clearly visible they did make an impressive sight for all whom could not help but be impressed or perhaps unintentionally somewhat intimidated.

Bertie would be ready for them as about a week prior he would receive an email from the respective gang's president requesting full use of facilities for their overnight stop. Due to the number of rooms then some members slept in a nearby guesthouse but they all converged upon the restaurant, bar and swimming pool for a relaxing time. Hey different strokes for different folks and Bertie would make the rules as Bertie saw fit. They would bring their own music which they requested to be played at full volume and in no time at all The Rusty Anchor became their playground. Bikers and gals would be in a confused dress code of leather and denim, boxer shorts, bras and panties and of course always one that would go swimming full Monty which Mir would look upon as slightly impolite to say the least. On these days Mir would work from opening time till well past her usual finish time as meals were in constant demand and Bertie was flat out making sure that no one was running short of a cold beverage. Yes, the unmistakable smell of good quality marijuana was present and so the hours slipped by and normally all would be retired by about 2am and catching some sleep before the next leg of their ride to Sihanoukville. Oh, for those of you who have taken a liking to Mir then Bertie would have sent her off home at about midnight with a nice little bonus for the extra time which she would have reluctantly accepted as she took her position seriously and if it was good enough for Bertie to be working long hours then as manageress, she would do the same.

Then following a hearty breakfast, the street would resonate to the signature sound that only Harley's can make as the waiting beasts came to life in readiness to carry their masters down the road to whatever lay beyond the horizon.

They were great nights and days due mainly to the blanket of respect and consideration shown to each other that on those occasions wrapped itself around The Rusty Anchor.

Now with that said, somethings and some people did not go un-noticed and one would have to be completely blind not to notice one of the bikers.

At first nothing seemed out of the ordinary. The same as normal with the arrival being just after midday, but amongst the arrivals was a lone rider of slender build and showed no problems in parking alongside the others. Well, you could have knocked Bertie over with a feather because when the helmet was removed and the dark wrap around glasses with the oval lenses pushed high on the forehead there standing before him was a fine figure of beauty, rough beauty, Bertie's kind of women. Her hair was as black as a raven's wing and hung down her back in a thick glossy platt stopping just short of her shapely and well-formed bum. An additional single finer platt the color of polished turquoise entwined itself from beneath her sunglasses, ducking and diving over and under the black platt travelling the full length of her hair, also finishing just shy of that increasingly attractive bum. She was clad in leather and denims with an amulet of bone and small stones around her neck, her hands were protected by short black gloves and extending up to the sleeves of her Tee shirt that had seen better days her forearms were tastefully tattooed. She wore no patch upon her back and showed no other means of identity. She moved with confidence amongst her friends as they unloaded their gear and tended to her own with no help being offered and it was clear that she expected none and needed none.

Cyrus the president introduced Bertie to the new addition, as she bore no sign of membership. Her name was Maia, obviously some South American, Aztec linkage there. Her handshake was strong and firm but not vice like. Maia was perhaps only a couple of inches short of Bertie's 6 feet and she faced him square on as she told him she was looking forward to her brief stay as she had heard many good things about The Rusty Anchor and the man that ran it. Mmmmm thought Bertie I owe Cyrus a beer for that leg up. That was all the time it took for Bertie to become fully and unintentionally focused on her deep and dark green emerald eyes and it seemed as if he was being drawn into some subterranean chasm from which there was no escape, but after what seemed an eternity Maia simply smiled and turned away and Bertie was no longer spiraling downwards. The spell, if indeed that is what it was had been broken.

He had to find out more and to some small extent he did as a couple of hours after their arrival Cyrus took Bertie to one side and explained that she had just turned up riding solo on her shiny hog, unannounced and unknown to any of the gang members. Cyrus had asked her several questions as to who she was and why was she there and she had simply but politely brushed him off and made herself comfortable in the guest's quarters. It was as if she had been there before but Cyrus certainly could not recall any such person during his fifteen years of tenure as president of the gang. Several other senior members tried to break thru this mystical barrier that shrouded her every movement and she rarely spoke but when she did then everyone present listened with keen attention as if captivated by this newcomer's presence. Later amongst themselves they would discuss what she had said but strangely no one really knew the meaning of her words, but they all agreed that their personal problems seemed to have become so much smaller well at least for the meantime. Who was this stranger who seemed so knowledgeable and understanding? Who was this one that goes by the name of Maia?

She paid her way and did her chores so it was decided that she could stay and besides she certainly added a definite alluring beauty to the surrounds unintentionally causing small amounts of anxiety and jealousy amongst several female members. A beauty and mystic that attracted several patched members to try their luck but to no avail as she was more than happy with her own company.

Maia emerged from her room and Bertie was susceptible to again being knocked over with that bloody feather. She had changed and now wore a short wrap around multi colored skirt of the finest cotton and a halter neck top of similar design leaving her finely tuned midriff exposed for I would suspect others besides Bertie to gaze upon with furtive glances. Her breasts were small but strained against the fabric of her top and could not go unnoticed. She had piled her hair high and was held in place by two attractive and uniquely hand carved combs, one of ivory and the other of ebony. Vine like tattoos began at her ankles and delicately climbed her long slender legs disappearing beneath the hem of her skirt without giving any hint or suggestion of where they ended. Maia smiled confidently at Bertie and chose to sit on the edge of the pool, content to watch her friends engage in their own form of water polo with a half-inflated ball that had appeared from who knows where.

Snap out of it, Bertie the beer stocks are running low. You do have a business to run and Mir had remarked that you seem to be spending more time poolside than you had on previous visits by the biker boys. Mir's observation was quite correct but in return Bertie had seen some exchanges of laughter and associated comments pass between Maia and Mir. Was there no one that was not affected by her radiant beauty and her confident but not overbearing demeanor?

The hours took their toll and slowly and some not too steadily on their feet they all retired. Mir had taken leave and Bertie had not seen Maia's retreat and so it was that he sat with his nightly cocktail. No help from Mr. Cohen this time, just sitting alone and silent and whether his eyes were open or resting the image of Maia floated before him and he felt an overwhelming presence of peace and tranquility. Who was this one that goes by the name of Maia?

With morning came the realization that Maia was nowhere to be found. Upon checking her room Bertie found it exactly as it would have been when Maia arrived, not a single thing was out of place and this was supported by the statement from the cleaning lady. Her bike was gone and when questioned the security guard claimed he had seen nobody leave. Well, he wouldn't have as he would have been fast asleep and his claim was about as much use as carting water in a bucket full of holes.

They ate their breakfast under a cloud of loss perhaps even disbelief and Cyrus summed it up when he addressed them all and said,

"She left as she arrived with no warning or explanation but we can all be thankful for her brief presence amongst us and none of us will forget the one we came to know as Maia"

Their departure was somewhat subdued, but still drew a crowd as they roared off down the main street and Bertie felt for sure that although unsaid Cyrus was hoping that somewhere up ahead on some vast stretch of open highway he would catch up with his strange and valued friend.

It was later that same day that Bertie was sorting thru some clothing up in his room when suddenly and startled he saw upon his bedside dresser two attractive and uniquely hand carved combs, one of ivory and the other of ebony.

Chapter 10

His loving and caring mother named him Reginald, but everyone knew him just simply as Reggie. Reggie lived in Thailand and had done so for the last twenty years or there abouts. He had actually lost count which does not matter and does not have too much bearing on what his part plays in this chapter or indeed the complete story, oh nearly forgot Reggie is Bertie's younger brother so that means Bertie is six years older than his sibling, simple arithmetic can you work it out? What are your strengths addition or subtraction? Then to make it easy I could give you either brothers age, oh you don't care how old they are. Well, let's just move along then as you are right it's not really that important.

From time to time and for no apparent reason he would cross the land border into Cambodia and come visiting and if asked why he would simply reply that it seemed a good idea at the time. The truth probably was that he welcomed the laid-back lifestyle that Korrup Kong and even Phnom Penh offered visitors, a good break from the bright lights hustle and bustle of both Bangkok and Pattaya. To add to that he had also self-claimed a chair at the front of The Rusty Anchor where he could often be found knocking back bottles of cold beer, consuming plates of French Fries that Mir would spoil him with, only to be interspersed with gagging on cheap cigarettes, Red Ara being his brand of choice.

It wasn't long before he struck up a friendship with Bart the Tuk-tuk driver. While brother Bertie was slaving away entertaining his guests and customers as only Bertie could, well Reggie would commandeer Bart complete with Tuk-tuk and they would visit a few of the less salubrious venues around the town.

Often when Reggie was in town Mir would suggest, tell, order Bertie to take a night off, join his brother and go for a walk around. It was on these nights that they would visit Henny up the track at the Cockadoodledo. Henny would rustle out the best of her brood to join them at the circular table in the beer garden and a great time would follow but pity the chick unaccustomed to Reggie's strange behavior that chose to sit close to and on the right of Reggie. After several cans of Klang it would seem as if his right arm had become instead a mechanical claw and additional beers acted like shots of WD40 freeing up this extension. Without prior warning it would reach out and encircle the friendly but now partly terrified hen, drawing the trembling bunch of feathers firmly onto his chest and locked like that they would remain long enough for Reggie to consume several more cans of Klang before heading off with said chick in tow to a secluded room located towards the rear of the main hen house. The claw for the most part was under control and no damage was ever inflicted. Although perhaps a little frightening for those encircled for the first time many did indeed seek the safety of the situation and roosted as close as possible to Reggie whenever he returned, keeping their spindly feet crossed tightly and hoping that Reggie would again be attracted to their smiling face and carefully prepared colorful plumage.

Mir was often suggesting to Bertie that he and Reggie should go up to Phnom Penh for a couple of nights as she assured Bertie it would be no problem for her to look after The Rusty Anchor and besides Bart and Harry would be on hand should the need arise to sort out any disruptive customers.

Bertie had total faith in Mir's honesty and integrity and so a date was set for the two brothers to test the water of Cambodia's capitol city. Both brothers had previously sampled some of what Phnom Penh had to offer but this was the first time in the company of each other.

Once squared away in a conveniently located hotel the two lads were out on the town. Well kind of, as Reggie was keen to revisit the Sitabout Bar and maybe catch up with conquests of past expeditions. Lead on McDuff thought Bertie and lead on McDuff was exactly what Reggie did to a small corner table in the crowded and smokey Sitabout.

Freelancers outnumbered the paying customers, who for the most part were happy to part with their dollars by buying drinks for pretty girls at pretty prices which led to negotiations for one might call less formal activities in the private rooms adjacent to the bar.

Only a short time passed before the good looks of both brothers attracted several hopefuls and so then there was four seated not too comfortably around the small table. Reggie was in his element and Bertie knew it wouldn't be long before the now dormant claw came to life, well ok for him but Bertie was uncomfortable squashed in with a lady perched half on a chair and half on his lap. You don't think that is possible well get yourself down to the Sitabout and in no time at all especially if you decide on the small table in the corner, you will be surprised at just how flexible some ladies can be when venturing after a drink and a squeeze of bottom or breast normally both but in no defined order. Yes, both cost money where do you think you are? the Salvation Army!!

Then suddenly as if by magic a women appeared, spoke briefly in Khmer which resulted in the prompt departure of the two new friends allowing the nearly captured and now clearly frightened to escape, and Bertie was finally able to stretch both legs before cramp set in.

The newcomer introduced herself as Fonnie. Fonnie was tall and had all the bumps in the right places and just maybe some of those bumps were not home grown, however early days to make such a prediction. Going on the speed that the two ladies had vacated the area it was clear that Fonnie was of some importance in and around the Sitabout. Her handshake was strong and her voice was unusual. It was high pitched but Bertie could still detect what could be described as a low growl that was unable to be completely hidden. Fonnie was one of those people that had developed the skill of introducing herself to strangers and at the same time making herself comfortable on a chair that had not formally been offered. So now there was three at the small corner table and Bertie thanked God or whoever else would listen that Fonnie had taken the chair closest to Reggie and on his right. Bertie mused to himself and wandered would the claw take on this new challenge.

No chance of that developing as both Bertie and Reggie were not mugs and it was becoming apparently clear that not so long-ago Fonnie had actually been Donnie and you know what that means. Reggie was in no way allowing the claw to take control on this occasion as under those tight blue denim shorts that Fonnie wore so well Reggie was sure he would find meat and two veggies. Perhaps it was the voice that altered frequently in pitch which was possibly caused by the slip of a drunken surgeon's knife when things of importance were being realigned. It had to be as everything else seemed to fit in this masterful disguise that would surely fool the most learned and the wise, but not Bertie or Reggie.

Hey there was no need to get angry or pissed off. We are what we are and Fonnie was bright and full of wit, a truly comical character but by no means a dumb and stupid character. The brothers were happy to buy her drinks and so a couple of happy hours of idle chat interspersed with games of pool none of which Bertie could win were spent at the small corner table in the Sitabout Bar. Reggie was not one for pool and Bertie said nothing but knew it was due to the mechanical workings of the claw, perhaps it needed to be inserted with an up-to-date microchip, or a few nuts adjusted with the aid of a three-inch spanner. The way things were developing if Fonnie spent much more time massaging Reggie's thigh, then there certainly would be some nuts that needed attention. Oh well we all have our own crosses to carry.

The gathering of three came to an end when Fonnie's phone rang and as quickly as she had arrived, she excused herself mumbling something about outside trade and was last seen exiting the rear door just to the left of the two beer fridges.

It soon became apparently obvious that Reggie needed to exercise his unusual but specialized and effective clutching appendage and not many minutes passed before safe and sound within the confines of the mechanical monster a lady of generous proportions was snuggled firmly against Reggie's chest. In customary style Reggie downed several more Klang beers then the duo up and headed out the back door zig zagging as they went like some deformed mud crab making its way to more safe, secure and private surroundings.

Bertie's wallet had its fair share of admirers so he did not sit alone for long, but politely declined several offers to head out the back as he was content to shoot a few games of pool and after finally winning a couple decided to call it a night and headed back alone to the hotel for some much-needed shut eye.

The brothers met for breakfast in the hotels dining room. Breakfast was a smorgasbord affair so Bertie was not surprised to see that Reggie despite one would think an adventurous and late night was already seated. Not only was he seated but he had made an honest attempt to get as much bacon stacked up on his main plate plus two smaller plates that were piled high and lined up waiting to be airlifted with the help of a three-pronged fork to the main cutting board where Reggie cut them into more sizable and manageable portions. Then with no further fuss or ceremony they were devoured and within a short span of time all three plates were empty and hardly needed to go thru the dishwasher. Yes, Reggie was partial to a rasher of bacon or three.

Bertie had been biding his time as there was no point in asking Reggie anything when he had a mouthful of bacon and both his hands were busy creating a short union between lashings of butter and a slice of toast, yes Reggie liked a bit of toast on his butter. Eating was an important event in Reggie's life but finally the opportune moment presented itself and Bertie asked about his brother's night and how did he get on with his new female friend. The answer was short and simple,

"Bertie, I got on as I always do right leg over first"

A wee bit abrupt perhaps but maybe towards the back of his throat there had been a collision between toast and bacon.

The bulk of the day was then spent bar hopping and people watching along the riverfront and only taking time out for a massage. A rather sad affair that turned out to be, despite the masseuses being friendly and full of smiles their skills left much to be desired. On a score of 1 to 10 then privacy during the rub down would be lucky if the combined score from the two judges managed to get above a 3. All that stood between each bed or let's rephrase that and put it in its correct perspective. All that hung between each bed was a flimsy curtain displaying a well faded maritime scene, more faded in some areas than others so much so that the octopus now only had three arms and the man-eating shark was missing all its front teeth. I guess this gave the punter something to study and think about as he lay on his back and got a frontal massage. I don't know, you tell me. There is no point in blaming the curtain as it had obviously hung there and done its duty for a considerable number of years and should have been retired some time ago. The poor and neglected curtain was tired, really tired which resulted in only the smallest hint of privacy being provided. Bertie was not one to support workers Unions, but there is always an exception and if that curtain had held a Union membership, then it would have been retired with distinction some years ago. It would have been free to enjoy the twilight years of life, free to hang out with other curtains of similar age and disposition in the park or Zoo, or any other place that curtains chose to hang about in during their last years, so not one size fits all.

The sun was setting and the light of day was fast disappearing, flashing neon's were now lighting narrow and roughly paved walkways, just enough to direct Bertie and Reggie to and thru the swing doors of Rose bar. Bertie's plan was to just have a couple then move on from bar to bar as any hint of staying could be construed as a suggestion for the claw to be brought into action. The plan worked exceedingly well for several hours, that is until they found themselves in a moderately lit and sparsely furnished Go-go bar. The central stage was an elevated walkway perhaps 90cm above the main floor and at each end was a shiny silver pole that extended itself to the ceiling above and on this walkway four pretty girls in scanty lingerie danced to some upbeat jive music, a 5th had managed to wind herself around one of the poles whilst still allowing for vertical maneuvers up and down its entire length. The seating area beside the walkway and at a lower level was fully occupied and each punter sat with head craned back causing various contortions of necks and could easily present an imaginary picture of turkeys at feeding time.

Whereas Reggie liked to settle in when out for a drink as previously discussed and described, Bertie was one for movement whether it be playing pool or dancing and without blowing his own trumpet, he had some years ago in the neighboring planet of Thailand done a bit of pole dancing at his local watering hole "The Hairy Pie" bar just off Soi 6 in the beachside town of Pattaya. It was there that each Sunday afternoon around about 2pm give or take an hour either way that a pole dancing competition was held. The competition was only open to foreign male visitors and thanks to some midweek coaching from one of the regular full time local pole dancing girls Bertie had come in 2nd winning the silver condom trophy on 3 occasions losing each time to some Latino whom several locals whispered to each other that the winner was really a lesbian making her way in the male environment of life. Stop right there!! because one could put forward an arguable case as to why men were competing in a pole dancing competition, but whatever it just didn't matter because Bertie was more than happy with his silver condom, as to him the first prize gold condom looked like it had recently returned from an exploratory trip up someone's rear passage. There was no 3rd prize not even the healthy end of a slow burning Cuban cigar was offered for those that missed out on first or second place.

Bertie was by now on his 4th whiskey chaser and feeling full of confidence he kicked off his sandals and climbed the five timber steps up onto the walkway. He performed several of his signature moves in time with the music as he made his way towards the far end, as he reached out and grasped the shiny pole, he was surrounded by the girls who quickly stripped him down to his boxer shorts, the ones with the elephants on front and back, he had bought them not so long ago as a matching pair with a shirt, which soon became his favorite shirt.

Mixed emotions and catcalls echoed around the bar. It was all on for young and old. Bertie's first and foremost thoughts was that no way was he going to be stripped of his boxers so up the pole he shot like a rat up a drain pipe and there he stayed hanging on grimly as he negotiated an agreement of surrender with the girls below. Yes, he would come down as they promised not to strip him naked. Fair is fair and so he performed a couple of ankle and knee hooks extending his body horizontally as he descended from the ceiling and then about eight feet from the timber floor, he pointed his feet upwards and came down head first. Fuck!! faster than he had anticipated and just before crashing he did recall that even while being coached up in Pattaya he had never been able to master the emergency stop on a downward fall. The girls gathered around and ice was poured by the bucket full over the crumpled form of the evening's unsuccessful entertainer and slowly and surely, he returned to his original form and was applauded by all in attendance. Reggie sitting in the corner wrapped in a tight embrace with yet another victim yelled something along the lines of,

"You will never learn"

The boys headed home the following day, this probably doesn't need saying but of course they departed only after Reggie had his breakfast of bacon and toast on butter.

All was well in order; Mir had done an outstanding job of looking after The Rusty Anchor and was quietly proud of the job she had done assuring Bertie that there had been no problems and certainly none that required the muscle from either Bart or Harry. Bertie made a mental note that he would place a bonus in all the staffs next pay packets and then got on with reading his incoming mail. He was not surprised to learn his friend Al would be arriving in a couple of days and as Reggie was homeward bound in the morning then he should have time to recharge his batteries.

Never a dull moment in Bertie's life and as one door closed another slammed in his face and he wouldn't swap it for quids, but had to admit he was still stiff and sore from his downward spiral on the shiny pole. Age was catching up as it does to all of us, but then maybe all of us don't try to relive younger days and go dancing up and down shiny poles.

Chapter 11

After seeing Reggie safely across the border Bertie headed back to The Rusty Anchor to catch up with himself prior to the arrival of Al. Midway thru the morning as he was sorting out staff bonuses his incoming mail alarm sounded and an email from Al arrived. The main purpose of the email was to say he was going to be a couple of days late, but could Bertie still hold the room and he would pay from the date of his original booking. The email went on to explain why he would be late and rather than you get the reasons 3rd hand I am going to cheat and simply print out Al's email so make of it what you will. I am sure he won't mind.

: Hey there Bertie…hope this finds you and your staff especially Mir healthy and happy. Sorry to say it looks like I will be a couple of days late can you still please hold my room and I will fix you up from original booking date, thanks buddy.

I am now in Vietnam with a couple of my old army pals Chuck and Herby and we are just revisiting some of our old "haunts" some are more pleasant than others as you can imagine. I often think of old Ben and wish he could be here with us as I know he would have a great time knocking around with us "young guys" and I know for sure Chuck and Herby would really enjoy his company. He really was a good old guy was Ben and I think you miss him as much as I do. God damn shame there weren't more like him, instead the world seems to be filling up with cocksuckers like the one we recently met that has kind of caused my delay.

A couple of night ago we three musketeers were knocking back a few sundowners in the local bar. An earlier night than usual for us as the following day we were going on a guided tour of one of the many tunnel complexes that the Viet Minh first built in their war against the French and were then expanded and improved by the Viet Cong which they used with great effect during the war. We were enjoying the company of a couple of friendly ladies; well Chuck and Herby were and although I reckon, I am better looking than those two for some reason I was on the outer. No problems I thought as will soon make up for lost time when I am over your way and get my arse up to Cockadoodledo. Here's hoping it hasn't burnt down in my absence, that would make Mir happy as I don't think she likes me going up there and she sure ain't too happy when I bring a chick home to roost for the night, but that Mir she is a diamond and you lucky to have her, huh and here's me telling you what you already know……

Anyway, at the other end of the bar was a big fat, loud mouthed Yank with a harem of several ladies all of whom were hoping for his attention but he was too wrapped up in his own importance letting everyone present and by the volume of his voice probably some locals in a neighboring province know that he had served as a special force operative and spent most of his time down in the tunnels seeking out and destroying the wee men in black pyjamas. Well buddy you haven't met Chuck or Herby but Chuck in particular had spent much of his time whilst serving in Vietnam with his head down those tunnels. As for me and Herby the only place we wanted to stick out heads was between the warm welcoming thighs of a local gal. Chuck's face said it all and what it said was the noise at the end of the bar was full of absolute bullshit. It did take some effort and persuasion on the part of Herby and myself to keep Chuck in his chair which in turn kept motor mouth safe from physical harm.

However next morning and who should join our tour party non-other than the fat fucker from the night before and his mouth was again in full gear just a bloody shame for all those present that his brain was not engaged. After a short and bumpy coach trip, we reached the site and were being given instructions from our guide who had been on the other side during the conflict and he had seen very little daylight as he had been a medic in one of the underground hospitals so the perfect person to send us on our merry way down into the poorly lit shafts leading who knows where. The fat fuck thought different and soon an argument developed between him and the guide resulting in him that had now become increasingly unpopular with everyone storming off shouting he would do his own tunnel exploring.

We all had a great day and then it was time to board the coach and head back for some cold refreshments. Yes, you got it in one the fat slug was missing, well I thought fuck let's go anyway but of course the majority on the bus were nice people so we began to search for our "best friend" It was no *surprise to me or Herby that Chuck returned to say he had located him that knew all about tunnels but strangely not enough to stop him getting stuck. This created great humor amongst everyone momentarily anyway, until Chuck went on to say that he was stuck, wedged in would be a better description down on the second level so it would be no easy extraction if we wanted to get him out in one piece. Did we want to get him out in one piece? Certainly, a subject that caused immediate debate and once again those nice people overruled what I was thinking.*

The learned heads of Chuck and our guide got together and it was decided that Chuck would enter from another opening and after reaching the second level it would be a short distance to cover and he would then find himself face to face with the problem and be able to provide him with some water and words of encouragement. I tell you now Bertie I was not keen on my mate going back down that tunnel as he is no spring chicken, getting on in years well no not as old as you but you are past old, you are now listed in the ancient bracket. Meanwhile the guide was busy arranging for rescue services to bring a small excavator and upon its arrival they would carefully dig down following combined directions of the guide and Chuck by way of handheld two-way radios.

Several hours later and well into the night with lights provided by a portable generator the rescue began in earnest. I will cut to the chase here and fill you in on details when I see you. Yes, we did rescue the idiot but had to laugh as that Chuck is full of surprises and as he was helping the poor soul to the ambulance it looked like Chuck stumbled resulting in a scream of pain from the useless one and it would have been painful as Chuck intentionally dislocated his shoulder. I guess Chuck was just making sure no more tunnel exploring for Mr. Know All.

Anyway, buddy must finish this as Chuck and Herby are keen to get out on the town, as now we are behind schedule so see you on 16th. Will let you know my time of arrival, perhaps you can be kind enough to get Bart or Harry to be at the bus station. Cheers I owe you a coldie or three. Take care, Al.

Bertie had no problems with Al's later arrival he was just pleased to know he was ok. His mates Chuck and Herby sounded like a couple of good blokes and maybe with a little luck Bertie hoped he would meet them in the not-too-distant future.

Having guests like Al around was a real pleasure but of course with the good came the bad and sometimes the ugly. Ugly was acceptable because at the end of the day beauty was in the eye of the beholder and who was Bertie to judge. His days of comparing with the likes of George Clooney or on a bad day Brad Pitt was water that had passed under the bridge of time quite a few years back now.

Remember how Bertie disliked the "plug in for a free charge up" gang well he had an equal dislike for those that thought bottles of water were exempt from and in bold print the message on the top of each menu that read "ONLY FOOD AND BEVERAGES PURCHASED IN THIS RESTAURANT CAN BE CONSUMED IN THIS RESTAURANT" That message, that warning is not difficult to understand but full credit to the marketing gurus that convinced huge numbers of the human population across the worlds wide expanse that it was absolutely necessary to be continually pouring that fresh stuff down ones throat. The lucrative result for those filling plastic bottles with water which showcased labels depicting clear mountain streams, crystal waterfalls and beautiful women or husky bearded outdoorsman was enormous. They did their marketing so well that now normal humans were frightened to leave home, even a short walk to the corner store could not be completed unless one took their water bottle as their closest and dearest companion. Sadly, there were many that not only thought but strongly believed that their water bottle attached to the hip or held tightly in either hand when placed on a restaurant table gave them right of passage to be exempt from common courtesy or observance of any establishment's rules.

Ha bloody ha The Rusty Anchor had news for them, although possibly not apparent till it became time to pay the bill but that glass that was supplied for them to drink from came at considerable cost. Often the customer would become quite agitated, an obvious rise in blood pressure, excessive sweating would not be uncommon and Bertie being the helpful and caring host would then suggest perhaps they should try a glass of water.........idiots.

Al certainly was not one of those and due to his caring nature and comical attitude we may well have lost him or at the very least seen him hospitalized. It was about mid-morning two days after his arrival on the 16th when Bertie heard the raised and high-pitched angry voice of Sena the cleaner, it was all in Khmer but its intent was obvious. Arriving at the scene Bertie found Sena in a crouched over position with the stringy end of her mop secure under her right armpit and the pointy end supported by her left hand about a foot from Al's throat. Al stood in his doorway seemingly naked except for the red stained pillowslip he held in such a way as to protect his manhood from at least a visual attack. Bertie slowly persuaded Sena to lower her weapon assuring her that all was ok, reluctantly she did just that and backed off but never removing her stare from poor old Al. Now that the impending physical attack was no longer a threat Al began to explain that the red stain was not blood as Sena had possibly thought but a splattering of harmless red wine carelessly spilled when he and the bundle of feathers he had brought home had got a bit frisky. He was not naked when he had approached Sena but wearing just a pair of boxers and holding the offending pillowslip out front, he certainly did appear so and things did escalate at a rapid pace. His sole and innocent intent had been to ask Sena how much extra money would she like for the extra work entailed in getting the stain removed.

Al returned to his room, Sena returned to her cleaning, Bertie returned to his office and swallowed a couple of Panadol and peace returned to The Rusty Anchor.

Chapter 12

Somehow several years have now slipped / passed by since Bertie first arrived in Korrup Kong. During those years the clouds of change had certainly spent considerable time hovering over and above the small border town that he now called home. The clouds had not been idle and the changes that were cast down although slow to take place had indeed reshaped the town and its citizens for better and for worse.

The recently opened industrial estate in close proximity to the town had provided many new jobs and with jobs came money and the things money could buy. Means of communication with the outside world were enhanced with improved internet access and smart phones of varying pedigrees, each brand providing its own assortment of features. The brightly colored pyjamas commonly worn by women going about their daily trips to the market or visiting friends had almost totally given way to a more western dress sense and this was blatantly obvious amongst those in their late teens and twenties often seen visiting newly opened beauty and hair dressing salons on their rostered days off from work on the estate. The older ones still preferring to dress traditionally and why shouldn't they?

The main street was never congested but certainly busier than when before the visible means of transport consisted of push bikes, older motorbikes and I kid you not the occasional elephant. These, yes bikes included, had been put out to pasture and now modern bikes still capable of transporting families of five at one time, late model cars and SUVs competed for owners' recognition and claims of importance and or personal wealth. The demand for these new toys more often than not required loans and was welcomed by banks and financial lending institutions and the collateral required by these 'friendly' pillars of the towns society was often the family home as the practice of borrowing relatively large amounts was new to so many. Interest rates were high and camouflaged and for the most part misunderstood by those that signed and thumb printed in triplicate the documents that in a short period of time resulted in repossession of the vehicle in question or worse still the family home. Of course, not everyone succumbed to the buy today pay tomorrow policy and the town prospered at a slow and steady pace.

It had never been Bertie's intentions to become involved in lending money but when Bart who was slightly smarter than the average bear approached him and rather timidly and very politely asked him if he would consider lending him $1000 to upgrade his Tuk-tuk then the seed was sown.

Bart had figured that Bertie's interest rates and loan conditions would be nowhere near as harsh as those of any bank and he was quite correct in his thinking. However, although Bertie had no intention of not lending the money, he let Bart know he would give it some serious consideration, about one weeks' worth and at the end of that week Bertie's easy and simple conditions and repayment plan became a binding document between two good friends.

That was the first of numerous loans to friends and associates of Barts most of whom were trying to improve their own small businesses. Each being of small amounts as one never knew when things could go pear shaped and if push did come to shove in someone refusing to repay amounts owed then Bertie really could find himself pissing into the wind trying to reclaim what was owed.

The small side-lined enterprise ran smoothly and repayments were made on due dates as no one wanted to upset the apple cart and have Bertie shut up shop resulting in no more easy loans as they would then feel the wrath of those that were hopeful in getting a future loan. Yes of course there always has to be one dickhead. Bertie hadn't really liked him from the first time they had met and when he baulked on his 2nd repayment Bertie had serious words with him. Somewhat foolishly in hindsight Bertie had gone to see him alone, words became heated and things turned physical and Bertie got a smack in the mouth with a short length of bamboo which required 4 stitches in his cheek and no repayments, well not right then but when Bart and some of his mates heard about it the offending culprit ended up with more than a few stitches and repayments as per agreement were resumed with no further hassles. Moral of that wee story is 'wake up Bertie you ain't as young as you used to be' and he did begrudgingly concede but only to himself that yep little more caution required at times of possible physical altercations.

With the improved buoyancy in the financial sector, it was to be expected that everyday prices would increase. Minimal were the increases but increase they did and Bertie's yearly medical was no exception. In order for him to hold a current work permit due to being a foreigner this was an annual requirement and it went something like this. Arrive at the designated clinic, be escorted by a female attendant / nurse to a vacant bed and rest for about ten minutes. The attendant would then return and take Bertie's blood pressure, once that task was completed, he would then be told the Dr will be there soon. So, a bit more time to relax, then he in the white smock coat with a stethoscope hanging from his neck would appear and introduce himself as the Dr for that day and ask Bertie if he felt ok or if he had any problems. At this point Bertie would assume he was referring to medical problems and would answer yes to the first question and no to the second. This would complete the in-depth medical examination and the good Dr would then advise Bertie to proceed to the front desk pay his $15.00 and receive a current medical certificate which qualified Bertie as being free of any physical or mental ailments and also included a multitude of possible diseases......it used to be only $13.50.

Korrup Kong was progressing but some practices were not made redundant and forgotten. This was apparently clear to all when one afternoon down the main street came a small procession. In the lead riding a motor bike was Snow White, even though his face was hidden by the helmet and visor that he wore there simply was no mistaking his characteristic slumped shoulders and protruding gut line which seemed to rest comfortably upon the bike's petrol tank. Next came a small flat deck truck and on the flat deck stood a local farmer with both hands firmly cuffed behind his back. To complete this small procession that was quickly gathering everyone's attention came one of Snow Whites dwarfs riding a motor bike which was towing a small two wheeled cart upon which was a water buffalo. A dead water buffalo and there was no need for any death certificate signed by the head of the Veterinary Association to be stapled to one of its horns as the open fly blown ragged cut that ran across its throat was plain to see making it obvious there would be no more wallowing in muddy puddles or pulling of ploughs for this poor beast.

Arriving at the roundabout the bike was uncoupled from the cart and replaced by he that had been released from his cuffs but then secured firmly to the cart and the gruesome load it carried. Several extra dwarfs had arrived and between them with the help of their batons they encouraged the guilty one to begin towing the cart towards the market square some fifty meters away. The market square had features common with many squares, that is to say it had four sides. Each side was about 80 meters long, stay with me now readers and together we will conclude that its perimeter measured about 320 meters in total. If you prefer to do the numbers yourself and got 320 then it's true, your arithmetic is improving.

The market vendors all turned out for this event and formed a gauntlet for the 320 meters and threw whatever rotten vegetables or animal's intestines that had passed their used by date at the convicted one as he struggled with every step towards the finish line.

Others made good use of their smart phones and captured in living color all that went before them. Well before the ordeal was over Bertie had seen enough and returned to The Rusty Anchor and some type of sanity and it was Mir that explained such punishment was not uncommon for those that stole and killed their neighbor's buffalo. The punishment was two-fold being both physical and loss of respect from the villages but it seemed to work as in the years that Bertie had resided in Korrup Kong this was the first time he had been witness to such a display of ancient and brutal justice.

Bertie still had regular talks with Henny over a cup of coffee up at the Cockadoodledo and although neither would admit it but deep down, they had become quite fond of each other. For some reason things had never developed past the cup of coffee stage, well maybe on a good day a biscuit or two could be added, perhaps just as well for both of their sakes. Henny had kind of moved with the times and had installed a good-sized fish pond out in the beer garden stocking it with multi colored fish of various species. She had also splashed out and freshened up the exterior of the dwellings / rooms with bright colors of yellow, red, blue and green. A weird mix of loud colors but somehow, they did seem to blend together, so yes Henny and her brood were a happy cluster of feathers.

The same could not be said for across the road at Anycockwilldo as Rooster could often be heard yelling and screaming at some unfortunate old boiler. His establishment had for the most part fallen by the wayside. His loud and continual outbursts of temper and general disregard for all around him began several months previously when his lover he /she or it had flown the coop with a customer and it was rumored was now living somewhere up north in a place called Siem Reap. Rooster had ventured up that way in an attempt to win back his one and only but came back alone showing severe signs of been given a right good pecking by some of the locals in the area so Rooster was far from a happy cockerel.

There was always maintenance or repairs to do around The Rusty Anchor and finally Bertie was able to start the largest of jobs currently on his "have to do" list. This involved giving the bamboo that lined the walls of the bar a light sanding and then two coats of semi-gloss varnish. This job Bertie was keen to do as no way did, he want to have a repeat of the stress and uncertainty involved in bringing another load down the river under the cover of darkness. Oh no once was enough thanks.

Mir had not been to work for two weeks and the reason for not turning up was genuine as she was well into her 8th month of pregnancy. Bertie had had a colossal battle convincing Mir that at this stage of her condition that home was where she should be. What a battle that had been as Bertie's knowledge of pregnant women was for all intents and purposes simply zero and every argument, he put forward was shot down in flames. That is until Bertie got clever, oh yeah Bertie got on the internet and educated himself on problems that could arise. Now the battle swung in his favor and finally he won but it was a conditional win and the condition was that Mir's sister would come and work in her place with strict instructions along these lines

"Don't let Bertie do any cooking because everything he cooks is sour"

Bloody hell who really does own The Rusty Anchor? Bertie mused to himself and chuckled quietly as he was more than happy with the state of play and atmosphere that tightly bonded Bertie, Mir and to a slightly lesser degree all the staff together creating a happy and vibrant place to be.

Mir's sister did a great job and it was she that arrived at work one morning bubbling over with the news that during the night Mir had given birth to a daughter.

Once the breakfast rush was over Bertie arming himself with an assortment of fruits and a small bunch of flowers turned up at Mir's bedside. Mir looked fine with a smile that ran from ear to ear but Bertie was kind of stunned. The ward was an open ward with perhaps 10 other new mothers and their babies, maybe not all new mums as perhaps some were on their 2nd or 3rd delivery but am sure you get the picture. Bertie had expected to see some type of incubator for the babies just like he had seen on some medical movies but instead each baby was beside their mother's bed and on a small table. Covering the baby was a framework of light wire which supported a type of muslin cloth which provided a fly and insect free environment for the newly born to come to terms with. Bertie found himself somewhat distressed by what he saw, but everyone seemed happy and who was he to interfere with the system that obviously although a little archaic worked and had worked successfully for a number of years.

Putting his feelings to one side he asked the usual questions as to how Mir felt and was there any problems;

"No problems Bertie, they cut me (which she demonstrated drawing her hand across her stomach) because I too small and take baby out, then sew back up"

Bertie wasn't expecting nor did he need to hear such an answer but that's how it was. Plain and simple and he was just happy and relieved that Mir and baby were ok. He did feel a bit awkward so busied himself cutting up some fruit then to his rescue but not intentional Mir's husband arrived and Bertie politely excused himself. Once outside he took a couple of deep breaths asking himself was the previous 20 minutes really real?

We now know that Bertie's knowledge of human evolution in particular and possibly the most important part that pregnancies and childbirth play in the scheme of such things was severely restricted. Therefore, we can forgive him for being totally surprised when Mir returned to work much sooner than he had expected. Her sister had done a great job but it really was great to have Mir back keeping guard on the kitchen and anything else she thought Bertie should stay away from.

So, it came to be that The Rusty Anchor was back to full strength. Guests came and went. Some were helped out the door and, on their way, earlier than they expected while others were pleased with the extra kind attention and happy disposition shown towards them by Bertie and his staff.

Chapter 13

Korrup Kong continued to grow and develop at a slow and steady pace which suited most that still called this once small riverside village their home. Educational and medical facilities were improving and the future shone brightly for those that had spent their first hours of life beneath a light wire frame supporting a muslin cloth.

From time-to-time visitors to Korrup Kong out walking late at night or in the wee small hours of a new day would pass by The Rusty Anchor. As they passed at first, they would hear the music and lyrics of Leonard Cohen's "First We Take Manhattan" A solitary figure seated outside and only partially seen in the shards of light that shone thru the not quite closed metal concertina door would invite them to join him and have a drink, if alcohol was not to their taste, then he would reach into the ice bucket and offer the newcomer a plastic bottle of water sporting a label of a beautiful women or a husky bearded outdoors man.

He would then smile and simply say;

"Let me tell you a story and it goes like this"

"His loving and caring mother named him Bertrand, but everyone knew him simply as Bertie"

THE END

HE WENT THAT WAY
Rupert Saville

*They were quite nice men and even helped me pack up
my unfinished doughnuts before escorting me off the
ferry and to the police station. I felt quite important
fancy sending two big policemen to take little skinny me
into custody.*

*Fire and Brimstone would best describe my bout with
the Wellington wrestler with no quarter given by either
of us. The cunt had a nasty habit whenever possible he
would hit me hard in the crotch area with his forearm,
unseen by the referee, perhaps. My balls were taking a
pounding and I started to feel quite sick at the base of my
stomach.*

*It was here that I really started to tell myself what a
fucking idiot I was. For all intents and purposes no one
really knew I was out here. I hadn't informed the police
in Alice Springs that I was going to hitchhike to Darwin.
I had no survival training etc. etc. in fact I had no right
or qualifications to be where I was, under a bloody bush
on the side of the Stuart Highway, deep in the Australian
Outback. Well like it or not I got myself in this mess, I
better damn well get myself out of it. If only I could keep
my mind centered on the positive, but because of my
weakened state it kept slipping into an abyss of negativity
and confusion.*

*There had been no physical connections until one
morning after Bruce had gone as usual at about 5am up
to the warehouse, Lottie came and sat on the edge of my
bed. Without saying anything she slid her hand under the*

*bed sheet and down the front of my shorts. Was I
shocked? Not really. Should I stop her? Of course, I
should. Did I stop her? Hell, no and that was the
beginning of our deceitful physical relationship.*

*Taking in a deep breath and trying to stop my stomach
churning at 100 miles an hour I approached the two
sentries. My first surprise was that these guys were by no
means big in physical stature, hardly my preconceived
idea of a Paratrooper but never did the phrase "you
can't judge a book by its cover" be more appropriate. I
introduced myself and presented my documents.*

*Quickly as possible I entered his room picked up one
of the tubular steel framed chairs and brought it
crashing down on his neck and shoulders, that certainly
stunned the cunt. Discarding the chair, I took him to the
floor and let rip with a volley of punches mainly in the
facial area, for Sergeant Budd's appraisal, before two of
his roommates dragged me off him.*

*Finding a dark secluded spot in the Dr's home-grown
vegetable patch we quickly got down to business and
were soon in the horizontal position between the Brussel
Sprouts and Cabbages.*

*I push him back and tell him to fuck off, it is then that
he pulls from his right pocket a flick knife and a four-
inch blade springs into sight. I scan the messroom tables
in search of a suitable weapon to defend myself but the
tables are all clear so I reach for, my only true friend
onboard.*

*On the street below, I pressed some money into her
hand, she insisted that it was too much but I told her to*

use the extra and buy herself some flavored milk. As I walked away my eyes held tears thinking of her returning to her room and perhaps being alone and unsure of what the next 24 hours, the next few days, the next week would bring. Certainly, a life of great uncertainty was the life Irene lived. I never did see Irene again.

All too soon and without saying a word the miserable face of the calendar and strongly supported by the low level of port wine suggested it was time for us to be heading home. We bid farewell to our friendly Kingfish promising them that one day we would return, set our sails and made passage back to the sights, sounds, hustle, bustle and confusion of Auckland, New Zealand's largest city.

I was very pleased with this outcome and the first chance we got we found and purchased a suitable engagement ring which I placed upon K's finger; however, this took two attempts as on my first attempt I selected the wrong finger, well with eight fingers to choose from a guy can't be blamed for not getting it correct the first time.

Walking Street stretched for about 800 meters and was a total mixture of Go-Go bars, discotheques, open bars playing music at full blast, many with live bands, seafood restaurants, street walkers of all shapes sizes and sexes, with many of the ladyboys looking just as pretty if not prettier than their female counterparts. Honest tourists just out to take in the sights mixed with drunks and druggies reaching out for that extra thrill, that extra excitement that would carry them thru until the sun rose and beyond. The street food sellers were doing a roaring trade and the gutters were clogged with food wrappers, plastic drink containers, vomit and dog shit.

I pointed out that the cabin staff had done a professional job of getting us safely off the plane and that the high standard that Qantas prided itself on carried all the way thru to both of them. I never did get the upgrade but I was more than happy with the final outcome and the respectful manner of all involved, certainly not forgetting the young lady with the knowing smile.

Should I go to Buriram and try to find Pai?

I was living a good life, a life I truly enjoyed and had been doing so for a number of years. I was being paid well and as Captain there were always challenges ahead some big, some small.

We began the search on 29th February, 2008 and first found the wreck of the Kormoran on 12th March, 2008 in about 2560 meters of water and approximately 112 nautical miles off the coast of WA. As can be imagined there was an intense air of excitement throughout our entire ship and this was soon intensified to the highest level when only four days later.

Printed in Great Britain
by Amazon

74919251R00072